NICOLE KIDMAN

BELOW: Nicole
Kidman relaxes
on Palm Beach,
Sydney, in 1994.

NICOLE KIDMAN

PAUL SIMPSON AND RUTH THOMAS

REYNOLDS & HEARN LTD
LONDON

Cover and inside images
© Rex Features

First published in 2003 by
Reynolds & Hearn Ltd
61a Priory Road
Kew Gardens
Richmond
Surrey TW9 3DH

A CIP catalogue record for this book
is available from the British Library.

ISBN 1 903111 39 0

Designed by James King.

Printed and bound in Malta
by Interprint Ltd.

ACKNOWLEDGEMENTS

Thanks to Emma Broe, Rod Edgar, Jenn
Fletcher, Andy Lane, Andrew Martin,
Adrian Rigelsford and David Pratt for
their assistance with the preparation
of this book, and to Marcus Hearn
and Richard Reynolds for their
patience and understanding
during a difficult time.

CONTENTS

PROLOGUE

THE attractive red-haired woman normally wouldn't have drawn too much attention. After all, in Los Angeles, everyone is used to seeing celebrities out on the street, doing their shopping and getting on with their lives. But then, when she leapt into the air, shouting for joy, it was clear that Nicole Mary Kidman really didn't care who saw her.

It was 8 August 2001 – and Nicole Kidman was soon to be a free and single woman once again. Six months of bitter recriminations, accusations and counter-accusations, and the pain of a miscarriage, were all forgotten for a moment as, for the first time since she came to America 12 years earlier, at long last her destiny wouldn't be linked with Tom Cruise.

A month later, chatting to British chatshow host Michael Parkinson, Nicole revealed that 2001 had been the weirdest year of her life.

Artistically, it couldn't have been better, with both *Moulin Rouge!* and *The Others* giving her some of the best reviews she had ever received. She had just gone into Capitol Studios to record an old Frank and Nancy Sinatra number with pop idol Robbie Williams, a recording which was destined to shoot to the top of the British charts. Yet, back in February, Tom Cruise's unilateral decision to divorce her – which she learned about only two days after their separation announcement claimed that there were no plans for divorce – had pulled the rug out from under her feet.

When the divorce was finalised on 12 November, Nicole Kidman knew she would have to start again. But that wasn't anything new for the girl from Sydney who had already grown from the gawky class giant into *People Magazine*'s Most Beautiful Woman of 2001...

OPPOSITE:
Nicole at the
London premiere
of *Birthday Girl*
in 2001.

GROWING PAINS

LISTEN to Nicole Kidman talking as herself, rather than in one of the many accents that she has perfected in her different roles over the years, and you could be excused for thinking that she's an Australian, born and bred. Indeed, Nicole always calls herself an Australian.

In fact, she holds two passports – Australian and American. When Antony and Janelle Kidman had their first daughter, they were based in Hawaii, where Kidman was researching breast cancer for the National Institute of Health. Nicole Mary Kidman was born in Honolulu, Hawaii, on 20 June 1967. Nicole spent most of her first four years in Washington DC as her father continued his research, pursuing his PhD in biochemistry. One of her earliest memories is of a snowball fight between her parents as she sat eating snow, DC suffering one of its normal cold snaps.

By the time her sister Antonia

ABOVE: The Kidman sisters – Nicole and Antonia.

was born, the three-year-old Nicole was developing a very strong will, and it was obvious to both her parents that she had a natural aptitude for singing and dancing. When they moved back to Sydney, and bought a house in the posh North Shore suburb of Longueville, not too far from the elite Lane Cove Country Club, it wasn't long before Nicole was enrolled for ballet lessons.

Acting wasn't particularly in Nicole's blood. Although her father appeared in a few amateur productions when he was at university, no one else felt the urge to stand up in public and perform. Risk-taking, however, definitely was, and it's something that Antony and Janelle Kidman instilled in their daughters from an early age. The family came as free settlers from Ireland in 1839, and one of Nicole's distant ancestors, a cattle baron named Sidney Kidman, ended up owning huge swathes of the outback and grazing hundreds of thousands of sheep. Her paternal grandfather was a gambler who won and lost fortunes, and Nicole also talks proudly of her other grandfather working on the Sydney Harbour Bridge's construction.

Nicole made her stage debut, aged six, in a Nativity play at her local school. The first year, she played the innkeeper's wife and remembers being "one of those terrible kids who said everyone's lines." The following year, she was one of the sheep, outfitted in a home-made costume made from a sheepskin car seat.

When Mary was rocking the baby Jesus, I went "Baaa, baaa, baaa," and of course everyone was in hysterics! This stupid kid's trying to upstage Jesus as a sheep! But I got a laugh, and that was it. I thought, "This is fun!"

Nicole was enrolled for mime classes aged eight, and two years later began Saturday morning drama lessons at the Philip Street Theatre in Sydney. By this time, she was already becoming very self-sufficient – a necessity in the rather unconventional Kidman household.

Antony and Janelle Kidman had very clear ideas of what they expected from their children. Janelle was an ardent feminist, and Nicole has often joked that her mother wanted to have a son, so she could bring up a boy in the feminist tradition. Janelle had no problem reconciling her feminism with her family role; to her, feminism was all about sisterhood – women helping other women. She tried to instil her beliefs into Nicole and Antonia but, when she banned Nicole from having a Barbie doll (other dollies were not a problem, but according to Janelle, Barbie was a sexist, male fantasy figure), Nicole promptly went and stole one from a local store. Realising that she couldn't expect a very small child to adopt all her own values, Janelle returned the stolen item, and bought one for her daughter.

Both parents followed left-wing causes, and a young Nicole Kidman could be found on the streets of Sydney handing out leaflets prepared by her parents.

My father was involved in the labour movement, and my mother was a feminist. And we lived in a conservative neighbourhood, so I'd get teased at school. Particularly because of the feminist stuff – that was considered really daggy. That's Australian for uncool.

Both daughters were expected to join in adult conversation from an early age, and current affairs would be discussed each evening over the dinner table. The girls weren't expected to be fazed by anything that happened. Janelle provided the girls with sex education movies when Nicole was 12 and, at the same age, her father took her to watch modern ballet routines, complete with naked male dancers.

The Kidmans wanted to ensure that their daughters had every opportunity available to them. Growing up, Janelle had wanted to be a doctor, but it just wasn't possible in the Australia of the Fifties and Sixties. Nicole thinks that's partly why Janelle has been so supportive of her daughters' chosen careers.

Australia is at least a decade behind the States in women's liberation, and when she was growing up, the most she could aspire to was nursing. Because of that frustration, she's been particularly supportive of my dream to be an actress.

While her husband continued his academic pursuits, Janelle worked every hour she could to ensure that her family didn't go short. That left Antony in charge of two little girls, who could probably look after themselves better than when he could.

My dad in the morning would make our sandwiches – disaster! All the other kids had their mums, who would make these beautiful little sandwiches and cut them. My daddy just put a slab of butter on top of bread and then "Whaddaya want? Peanut butter?", wouldn't cut it, and wouldn't wrap it properly, so by the time you opened it at school, it was all stale, and all the kids would tease us.

Both parents encouraged Nicole to widen her horizons. As the young girl reached her teens, she was learning all about both the real world and the worlds of the imagination. She was learning Latin at school, and enjoyed reading anything she could lay her hands on. Aged 13, she read *War and Peace* for the first time and found herself identifying with the heroine Natasha. So much so that it spurred her on to follow her dream of being an actress. Anything that would take her away from the real world, where her growth spurt to 5' 10" by the age of 11 left her feeling an outsider among her classmates at North Sydney High, some of whom nicknamed her 'Stalky'. Her fair skin and carroty hair made her feel that she was one of the ugliest people in the world, and that belief can only have been confirmed by an experience at summer camp when a boy had to be dragged screaming across the floor to ask her to dance. Nobody seemed to want to spend time with her.

Nicole's solution? While her neighbours and classmates were heading for Sydney's beaches, she would spend her weekends at the Philip Street Theatre, sometimes being the only person there on a bright sunny afternoon. She was teased about the amount of time she spent there, but she thought it was fantastic. She had her first kiss onstage, as well as an introduction to some other more unusual sexual practices in her professional stage debut – a production of Frank Wedekind's *Spring Awakening*, about sexual repression in the late nineteenth century.

I had to yell "Beat me! Harder! Harder! Harder!" every night... My grandmother was looking after us. She really liked it.

ABOVE:
The Kidman family:
Antonia, Janelle,
Antony and Nicole.

Nicole's talents were recognised at a very early age, and director Jane Campion, who would later direct Nicole in *The Portrait of a Lady*, desperately wanted her to appear in a short student film that she was working on. North Sydney High's headmistress intervened, saying that Nicole needed to concentrate on her exams, and much to the budding actor's annoyance, she wasn't allowed to participate. Campion promptly sent her a postcard, telling her to "protect her talent" and hoping that they would get a chance to work together at some point in the future. Campion wasn't the only student director to be turned down: P J Hogan, who would later helm *Muriel's Wedding* and *My Best Friend's Wedding*, also tried unsuccessfully to involve Nicole.

It's one thing to turn down a student film, but professional work was something else. While many actors cringe if someone catches their early films, Nicole Kidman doesn't have the option, since one of her first, the uplifting TV movie remake of the 1947 movie *Bush Christmas*, turns up every year on Australian television. Another early effort, *BMX Bandits*, also regularly plays on cable channels around the world.

When she was 14, Nicole met a director/producer who would change her life. John Duigan emigrated to Australia in 1961, and was rapidly establishing himself as one of the country's leading directors. After leaving the University of Melbourne, he originally planned to act and write, but instead found himself directing low-budget films with a government grant. His two films *Mouth to Mouth* and *The Winter of Our Dreams* brought him to public attention, and established him as a director with a subtle eye for cultural and political details. Duigan was casting a children's television drama and auditioned the young Nicole, whose talent he immediately recognised.

> I first met her at an audition when she was 14. She was several inches taller than the other girls and had this great shock of red hair. But she was remarkably poised and very smart. She got to the kernel of things without pussyfooting around.

Duigan cast her in a number of TV movies and, at the same time, Nicole was modelling for magazines like *Dolly*. At a modelling job one weekend, a stylist took it upon herself to alter Nicole's look, tinting and revamping her hair. Gone were the wiry locks that Nicole had been trying to blowdry into submission, and on the Monday she arrived at school with a head of bright red curls. It was as if the ugly duckling had suddenly become the swan.

Eventually, buoyed by her success, Nicole decided to leave home. She wanted to be an actress, and knew she wasn't going to be heading to college and following the academic route.

> I wanted to cut loose. I was a nightmare to my parents. I lied to them. There was a time when my mother said, "I can't live in the same house with her." It wasn't all roses. But that also put me in good stead. Because I grew up in a family that yelled a lot, I don't cower. People would lose their tempers in our house, things would be thrown, and an hour later we'd sit around and have a laugh.

ABOVE: The *BMX Bandits* ready for action.

The opportunity to make the move came when she was cast in the Disney TV series *Five Mile Creek*, which was filming for seven months in Western Australia. Nicole dropped out of High School and went to pursue her dreams.

OPPOSITE:
A freshfaced future star poses for the camera.

FLYING THE COOP

FIVE MILE CREEK was a turning point for Nicole. Spending so much time continuously in front of the cameras, her awkwardness fell away and her camera technique blossomed. She was now in a position to be more choosy about the roles she accepted, though she recognised that sometimes she might have to work on material that didn't show her at her best.

One such movie was *Windrider*, which premiered at Christmas 1986. Nicole played Jade, the girlfriend of P C Simpson, an enthusiastic surfer. Life eventually imitated art, and Nicole fell in love with the ten years older Canadian-born actor Tom Burlinson, who played Simpson.

I accepted roles when I was younger which I don't regret, because on everything I've done, I've learned something or I've met someone who's been quite instrumental in moulding my career. On *Windrider* I met someone that I had a relationship with for three years, which was really important to me and helped me to grow. So you've got to look at things positively. I did do some things that weren't of really high quality, but I learned a lot.

Burlinson wasn't Nicole's first boyfriend. She remembers really starting to notice boys when she was about 14 years old. And when she was 16, she took the money that she had saved up from her acting career to date and decided to tour Europe, arriving in Amsterdam with 3000 Australian dollars and a Dutch boyfriend twice her age. She soon found herself single again when she suggested that they should just be friends. Unsurprisingly, he wasn't willing to go along with the idea ("I naïvely did not understand male sexuality at that age," Nicole commented wryly a few years later), and they parted company.

While she was travelling, Nicole found what was to become a very treasured item when she was wandering round an Amsterdam flea market. It was a very simple but very beautiful antique brocaded gown dating from the 1930s, which she would eventually wear at her wedding to Tom Cruise. As with so many things in her life, Nicole knew instantly that this was right for her and she bought it for safe-keeping. She soon headed back to Australia when her money ran out, but not before spending a few nights in a tiny attic room in Paris and visiting Florence in Italy, where she witnessed the town's first snowfall in 18 years.

Shortly after arriving back in Australia, and starting work on *Windrider*, Nicole received some news that shook her to her core. Her mother Janelle was diagnosed with breast cancer. Nicole moved back home as soon as she could, and took most of the next year off to help her mother.

Suddenly the person you love most in the world is losing her hair and sobbing every night. It was very hard on me and it still remains a big thing in my life. It was very hard to see your mother going through such pain. It was a really terrifying time. It opened my eyes to mortality, to pain and suffering…

Nicole wasn't simply a moral support to her mother during this time. During what she still describes as a "year of hell", Nicole took a professional massage course to help ease her mother's pain. Because of the intensive chemotherapy and radiation therapy that Janelle required, all her back muscles would tighten up. Each night Nicole would stretch her mother out on her bed and try her best to massage the tension away.

Janelle's illness had a long-term effect on the Kidman family. Although their mother recovered, both Nicole and Antonia are aware that statistically they are at risk from the disease. Nicole has become a staunch supporter of the UCLA Women's Reproductive Cancer Program, realising that she is in a good position to give something back.

The effect on Antony was more dramatic. Having suffered through his wife's illness, he shifted the focus of his work so that more help would be available to other sufferers from the disease. During the 90s, he worked on a major clinical trial on the effects of cognitive behaviour therapy on women with advanced breast cancer, and has since become renowned for 'self-help books' designed to assist cancer patients and their families in coping with the disease.

Although Nicole wanted to spend as much time as she could helping her mother, her creative juices still needed an outlet. When she was publicising her major singing role in *Moulin Rouge!*, Nicole recalled that, when she was 17, she was in a band in Australia – "and we didn't do well."

John Duigan hadn't forgotten the redhead whose career he had helped to launch and, when he was casting the epic miniseries *Vietnam* for Kennedy Miller Productions, he brought Nicole in for a six-and-a-half-hour improvisational audition. Nicole came through with flying colours and was cast as Megan Goddard, one of the central characters in the series' Australia-based segments. Megan is first seen as an awkward schoolgirl in the Sixties and, as the ten hours of the series progress, she becomes a free-thinking young adult protesting against Australia's involvement in the Vietnam conflict in the early Seventies.

Nicole was certain that *Vietnam* would be a success, both as a series and also as a showcase for her talents. She had confidence in Duigan's work and knew that Kennedy Miller had an international reputation as a result of the *Mad Max* films with Mel Gibson. She screamed with joy when they called to offer her the part because she knew that finally, after years of playing 'the girlfriend', she had a role she could sink her teeth into: there were comic scenes, dramatic scenes and everything inbetween. Nicole knew that the more preparation she could do, the more realistic she would be – a guideline she's followed to this day.

> It really made a difference to me to work with a three-dimensional character and flesh out the comic and dramatic aspects of the role. I became obsessive about acting. I did all sorts of research about the mores and culture of the 60s. I wasn't even born yet when the Beatles became popular so I had to sit down and study life in the 60s, as if for a term paper. And from there on, there was never the slightest doubt about the path I was going to follow. Win or lose, I was going to stick with acting.

Kidman's performance was so strong, she won the Australian Film Institute's Award for Best Performance by an

Actress in a Leading Role in a Television Drama, as well as a Logie Award from Australian *TV Guide*, an accolade voted for by viewers. One scene in particular stood out and was to have a major effect on Nicole's future career: Megan is protesting against conscription on talk-back radio. As she does so, her estranged brother, who has only just returned from Vietnam, calls in and she breaks down listening to his voice. "There wasn't a dry eye in the country," director Duigan firmly believes.

It was a tough scene for any actor to play, and even more effective because Nicole was still only 18. The six-minute scene focused almost exclusively on her face and her reactions as she went from protesting to listening – and then recognition. To her pride, Nicole did it in one single take.

Nicole enjoyed filming the miniseries. She was still dating Tom Burlinson, and was loving her young adult lifestyle. She had her own apartment and was able to be as domestic as she wished. While her parents might still have been disappointed that Nicole wasn't going to head to college, they accepted that she needed to follow her dream and were very supportive of her. Unlike many parents of a teenage daughter, they weren't shocked by Nicole's relationship. "My mother would always say, it's not age, it's people," Nicole recalls. "He was the one who gave me a great belief in men. He was kind and open and gave me a lot of freedom. And because he was so much older, he realised that I probably wasn't going to stay with him. Most men that age would have been insecure and controlling. I was really lucky to have had him."

The young Nicole also dabbled in the drugs scene at the periphery of the film world. However, she was soon put off when her mother pointed out the effects that the drugs would have on her body, and how many brain cells she was destroying every time she dabbled.

At this stage, Nicole seriously considered heading to Australia's prestigious National Institute of the Dramatic Arts, the equivalent of Britain's RADA, following in the footsteps of her famous countrymen Mel Gibson and Judy Davis. However, when she discussed the idea with John Duigan, she was quite surprised to find that he was extremely opposed to it. Duigan was sure that whatever spark it was that set Nicole Kidman apart from other actors could easily be quenched in the training that NIDA provided.

He said "Don't you dare go – they will destroy you!", so I never went. I always think I would have loved to have gone because I love being around actors. I love talking about acting and I wanted to go to college, but he said, "Don't go," so I chose the other route – which was to work, work, work...

And work she did. As *Vietnam* went through the labours of post production and eventual transmission, Nicole worked on small roles in the made-for-TV karate thriller *Nightmaster*, in which she was able to demonstrate her natural athleticism in a number of scenes set in a gymnasium, plus *The Bit Part* and *Un'Australiana a Roma* (An Aussie Girl in Rome), in which she worked for Italy's master of exploitation pictures Sergio Martino, director of *Prisoner of the Cannibal God* and others.

Nicole was confident that *Vietnam* would open doors. If it didn't, she knew that she would probably just coast along for a few more films before disappearing off everybody's radar. But open them it did – when Kennedy Miller began production on their new thriller, *Dead Calm*...

RIGHT:
On the brink of stardom - Nicole pictured in Sydney, Australia, in February 1989.

DEAD CALM

I N the period between *Vietnam* and *Dead Calm*, Nicole gave a couple of performances that would resonate throughout her career. In *Emerald City*, for which she was nominated for another Australian Film Institute Award, she appeared for the second time opposite Australian actor Chris Haywood, playing a girl who appears to be with her man only for his money. Yet when the chips are down, she still supports him. As she was to experience all too often, Nicole herself would soon be dismissed as just 'Mrs Tom Cruise' by those who wished to ignore her talents.

She also returned to the Sydney stage to appear in *Steel Magnolias*, playing the role that Julia Roberts would essay on screen. It was to be the last time that she would have the opportunity to experience a live audience until her tour de force in David Hare's *The Blue Room* in London and New York a decade later. Around this time, she filled in as an usher at Sydney's Capital Theatre – and on one unfortunate occasion found herself cleaning up the mess in the latrines.

All the while, she was steadily pursuing her goal of stardom. She knew that she couldn't sit around waiting for someone to present her with dream roles on a platter. "I think you deserve what you work for," she says bluntly, "And I was willing to work hard."

Although Nicole was unaware of it at the time, her performance as Megan

ABOVE: Rae and John Ingram (Sam Neill) are wary of their uninvited guest in *Dead Calm*.

18

in *Vietnam* had impressed the series' producer Terry Hayes so much that there and then he decided he would write the lead role in his company's new thriller, *Dead Calm,* for her. He was so convinced that she was the right person for the part that he persuaded his colleagues at Kennedy Miller to watch her radio station scene in *Vietnam,* and then cast her in the role even when bigger names such as Debra Winger and Sigourney Weaver were being mooted.

Dead Calm had an interesting voyage to the screen. It was based on a 1963 novel by Charles Williams, which had originally been optioned for filming by Orson Welles. The veteran Hollywood director cast Laurence Harvey and Jeanne Moreau in the lead roles of John and Rae Ingram in his version, which he retitled *The Deep.* Unfortunately, Harvey died on location and the project was shelved. It took some years of negotiation for Kennedy Miller to convince Welles' de facto widow, who controlled the rights, to allow them to proceed.

In Philip Noyce's film, Nicole plays Rae, the wife of surgeon John Ingram. Following the gruesome death of their young son in a car accident, they embark on an extended yachting trip as therapy for the traumatised mother. Everything seems to be going well, with Rae starting to come out of herself, until the couple rescue Hughie Warrinder, the sole survivor from a sinking schooner near the Great Barrier Reef. Warrinder claims that all the other passengers died from food poisoning, but when John Ingram goes to investigate on board the schooner, he realises that this is far from the truth.

The film then follows two separate plotlines, Ingram struggling to survive when he is trapped in the hold of the sinking ship (with the water rising rapidly), while Rae finds herself equally trapped with Warrinder on board her own yacht. Rae has to snap herself out of her melancholy distraction and outwit Warrinder, trying to gain his confidence before eventually attacking him with a harpoon gun and going to save her husband.

Nicole knew that this was another big opportunity. If she didn't find a part in which to shine, the opportunity that *Vietnam* had given her would be wasted. She threw herself into the role, focusing all her energies into persuading audiences worldwide that although she was still only 20, she could believably play the wife of a 36-year-old man – a mother who had just lost a five-year-old son. Cast opposite Sam Neill as Ingram and Billy Zane as Warrinder, Nicole had to provide an electrifying performance of her own – and she succeeded magnificently. One bit of scripted dialogue – "Captain Ingram, your daughter is just through here" / "She's not my daughter, she's my wife" – was edited out of the movie when the producers realised that the relationship between her and Neill was clear.

As with everything in Nicole Kidman's life, her breathtaking performance came about through hard work, rather than luck. As soon as she was cast, she worked with a voice and movement coach so that she had the sound and posture of a woman in her mid-twenties. She even went on location to Hamilton Island in Queensland a month before filming began so she could learn to sail the 80' yacht on which most of her scenes were filmed. She set out to meet navy wives and mothers, and mothers who had lost children, so she could make sure that all her reactions were genuine.

I concentrated very much on trying to imagine what it would be like to lose a son. And I succeeded. I woke up from a dream, about a week before we started shooting, believing – really believing – for that two seconds or so when you're not sure whether it's a dream or reality, that I had my own little boy in bed with me. When I had experienced that amazing maternal feeling, I could then work on imagining losing that.

The filming was difficult. In fact, according to everyone involved, it was a nightmare. Cast and crew spent over three months living on the hot and sticky Hamilton Island, filming from dawn to dusk. Even though they had done their research, nothing could prepare the cast for the brutal conditions brought on by the filming. Although Nicole had experienced a lot of challenges on her earlier films, they paled by comparison to what was expected of her in *Dead Calm* – action, humour, pathos, and even a seduction scene that was rape as far as her character was concerned. Through it all, thanks to Dean Semler's inspired cinematography and Philip Noyce's skilled manipulation of the audience, Nicole shines as a beacon of hope.

Nicole knew that she was working with considerably more experienced players than herself and made sure she took every opportunity to improve her skills. Philip Noyce was constantly amazed by the way she always took direction and tackled whatever was asked of her with a youthful enthusiasm that communicated itself to the more seasoned cast and crew around her. She simply focused all her energies on the part, making sure that she was well-rested before shooting began so that she could give her best.

Even the rape scene, where she was nude on screen for the first time in her career, didn't worry Nicole.

I have no hang-ups about that. The real focus of that scene is on my face, not my body, where we see the rape through her reactions, her mind.
I did it instinctively. I don't like rehearsing. I want spontaneity.

And if the cast worked hard, they also played hard. Noyce didn't want any off-screen friendship between Nicole and Billy Zane to spill over into the film, so subtly encouraged the two of them to spend time apart. While Zane was living up to his hell-raising image, Nicole would be tucked up in bed by 10.00 pm. The two actors almost had an unspoken agreement that they wouldn't get on, so they didn't – even though Nicole later admitted that she wished she had been able to let loose a bit more than she did.

That didn't mean that Nicole didn't have any fun. Come the weekend, she and Sam Neill would up and let their hair down at the local nightclub.

Everyone used to go dancing and drink heavily and do all of that. And he loved it cause I'd take him out and they'd play Sixties music, and because of *Vietnam* I'd learned to do all the Sixties dancing, and he was just bowled over by that. So then he'd ring me up and he'd say, "Nic, let's go out dancing," and so I'd take Sam out, and all the girls at the bar would be like, "Sam Neill, Sam Neill, my god, that's Sam Neill!" And he just goes wild and dances.

Dead Calm gave Nicole the opportunity she needed to show the different facets of her acting.

ABOVE:

Rae Ingram faces terror on the high seas in *Dead Calm*.

The introverted, almost emotionally catatonic figure of Rae is forced by circumstances to come out of herself and, by the end, is revelling in the destruction of the man who has tried to come between her and her husband. Everyone who saw her striking performance – and the image of her with her flaming red hair billowing in the sea breeze, jaw locked in steely determination – was bowled over. The critics agreed that she excelled. "Kidman and Zane do generate real, palpable hatred in their scenes together," wrote Roger Ebert, while Desson Howe praised her "sensitive portrayal" in his *Washington Post* review. The review that probably pleased Nicole most was Rita Kempsley's, also in the *Post*: "While she tries our patience, she never loses her appeal."

The film's strong performance at the American box-office meant that Nicole embarked on a lengthy press tour to promote the movie when it opened worldwide. She was very conscious that the film industry is a fickle business and that, though Warner Bros were providing suites, massages and

fancy cars while she was still flavour of the month, that situation could change at any minute. When she returned to Australia to promote the film, she still drove her mother's "old bomb of a car", concerned that, if she became too attached to all the luxury that was surrounding her, she would lose her sense of who she was; a self-awareness she still displays today.

It was becoming increasingly clear to important people in the film industry that Nicole Kidman was someone to watch closely. She had more than justified the faith that Terry Hayes and Philip Noyce had shown in her when they decided to take the risk of not having a 'name actor' in the starring role. Interviews in the press compared her favourably with Mel Gibson, another Australian actor who had taken Hollywood by storm, while Noyce went so far as to claim that he didn't think Nicole's potential had any limits.

With all this attention, it wouldn't be too long before Nicole herself would become the 'name actor' on a movie. In November 1988, six months before *Dead Calm* opened, legendary Hollywood agent Sam Cohn flew to Los Angeles to meet with her. Following a breakfast meeting with her, he became her American representative, adding her to the ranks of Meryl Streep, Sigourney Weaver and Woody Allen, based on the strength of her performance in *Vietnam*. Nicole knew that if she was serious about her craft and her career, she would need to tackle the American and world markets – otherwise she would be stuck in Sydney for the rest of her life.

She didn't need to worry on that score – for one of the fans of her performance in *Dead Calm* was a certain Thomas Cruise Mapother IV...

DAYS OF THUNDER

WHEN she looks back on her younger days – before she was drawn across the Pacific into the arms of Tom Cruise – Nicole Kidman seems to have few regrets. It was a time when she could cheerfully take risks and just see what happened. While she was filming the TV miniseries *Bangkok Hilton* in the summer of 1989 (for which she collected her second Australian Film Institute and Logie awards), she took the opportunity to visit a blackmarket snake farm in Thailand. In a forerunner of the many dangerous sports with which she has occupied her time subsequently, she let one of the boa constrictors entwine itself around her neck. Nicole would become entwined in a different sort of grip later that year, when Hollywood beckoned.

Although *Days of Thunder* is now best known as the film on which Tom Cruise and Nicole Kidman got together, she was only invited to audition for a role based on her performance in *Dead Calm*. Nicole had met Cruise briefly in a London restaurant a few months earlier but admits that she wasn't particularly impressed by him. "He had no hair, and he didn't look like such a babe," she recalls. Cruise was in the middle of filming his harrowing role as Ron Kovic in *Born on the Fourth of July* and was definitely not at his physical best – whereas Nicole was shining from the glow that success brings. As Cruise himself later admitted, it was most definitely lust at first sight.

Nicole was at a film festival in Japan when she first heard that Cruise was interested in meeting her for *Days of*

Thunder. She didn't get her hopes too high; she had already been over to auditions in Hollywood, and therefore knew that there was a good chance she would audition and not get the job. But at least it was a free trip to Los Angeles. Her plans initially were to go to her meeting, get together with *Dead*

ABOVE:
As Katrina Stanton
in *Bangkok Hilton*.

Dr Clare Lewicki and Cole Trickle (Tom
Cruise) at the race course in *Days of Thunder.*

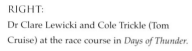

ABOVE:
Dr Clare Lewicki
ponders an
unprofessional
relationship in
Days of Thunder.

Calm director Philip Noyce and his
family at the Chateau Marmont, then
head off to visit her sister in London.

The meeting didn't seem to start off
that well for Nicole. She didn't feel
fantastic, since she hadn't had a chance
to recover from her flight across the
Pacific, and felt very embarrassed
when she realised the height difference
between her and her potential co-star.

> When Tom stood up and we shook
> hands, I found I was looking down
> at him. It wasn't that he was so
> short, it's more that I'm so tall.
> I knew it simply wouldn't do,
> having the girlfriend tower over
> the macho race-car driver.

Nicole didn't really rate her chances of
success, particularly when she noticed

that the other men in the room were all
staring at the slightly odd spectacle of
her looming over Cruise. After giving
her a couple of test pages to read, the
producers explained that they didn't
have a specific role in mind and
thanked her for her time. Nicole was
prepared to write the meeting off to
experience, so was very surprised
to receive a phone call the next day
offering her the part. When she queried
the height differential, she was told
simply, "It doesn't bother Tom, so it
doesn't bother us."

At that stage, Nicole began to fall
for Tom Cruise. She admired his self-
confidence and his ability to inspire
confidence in others. She also admired
men who would go out with women
who were taller than them and weren't
self-conscious about it. At the back of
her mind, she also recognised that this was
a rare opportunity for an Australian actress
and she needed to grab it with both hands.

Contrary to myth, Cruise and
Kidman didn't spend the entire shoot
of *Days of Thunder* gazing adoringly
into each other's eyes, even if Nicole
admits that her first reaction when she

shook Cruise's hand at the audition was "Ooooh!" Cruise was in virtually every scene of the film, playing Cole Trickle, a cocky young stock-car racer who gets an opportunity to challenge the top racers. Helped by veteran former driver Harry Hogge (played by Robert Duvall) and Nicole as beautiful neurosurgeon Dr Claire Lewicki, Trickle develops a rivalry with veteran racer Rowdy Burns as he goes through a dramatic process of self-discovery. And smashes a lot of cars up along the way.

Nicole's scenes didn't begin filming until some time into the shoot, which started in November 1989 at Daytona, Florida. Screenwriter Robert Towne had rewritten the part to fit her, although she later dismissed it as being very similar to the sorts of roles she had been playing in Australia since she was 16. She felt she had already outgrown being 'the girl friend', albeit, in this case, a very bright one. It was the first time that Nicole played a brainy scientist, but by no means the last. "I wish I had a better role," she would later comment about her all-important first American movie. "It was kind of one-dimensional."

Nicole had to spend a lot of time hanging around the location, and had the opportunity to get to know her co-star in all his various guises. She recognised that, if he hadn't become an actor, Cruise would almost certainly have become a professional car racer, sensing in him a similar attitude to risk-taking. Cruise's interest in racing had been piqued when he worked on the film The Color of Money with Paul Newman, and by this time he had actually raced professionally. Nicole's attitude couldn't be more different: she didn't know one car from another and frankly couldn't care less. She described herself as a lousy driver and

hadn't even seen a car race before working on Days of Thunder – and didn't feel that it was a part of her education that was sorely lacking.

But Cruise's passion attracted her. Since the film was clearly very special to him, and there was a lot of money riding on the outcome, he was willing to spend however long it took to get a scene right.

> Tom was cool and unflappable, and very giving as an actor, not afraid to open up and show his emotions. He's tough on himself but generous to his colleagues. He'll do as many takes as necessary to get it right.

This sat well with the girl who had refused to co-operate with a prestigious documentary team in Sydney a few months earlier when they had requested her to do some 'fake' acting. The attraction between Cruise and Kidman began to grow, with Cruise taking her for a spin around the Daytona racetrack at 180 mph and spending more and more time with her.

There was only one problem. Tom Cruise was a married man, with what appeared to be a very peaceful marriage to fellow actor Mimi Rogers. As a result of his roles in Top Gun, The Color of Money and Rain Man, Cruise had a considerable following, and the paparazzi were always interested in what he was up to. Until Nicole arrived in his life at Daytona, there had been little for them to report – but now his white BMW or Harley-Davidson motorcycle could often be spotted outside Nicole's Daytona Beach condo.

In fact, appearances were deceptive. Cruise's marriage was already in trouble before Days of Thunder began filming. Cruise and Rogers had lifestyles that were becoming increasingly incompatible: he

ABOVE:
The world's oldest
high school girls?
Nicola Radcliffe and
Thandiwe Adjewa
(Thandie Newton)
prepare for the
world in *Flirting*.

enjoyed racing cars, she would rather spend the time in a Beverly Hills boutique. Without making a song and dance about it, Cruise had officially separated from Rogers and then filed for divorce, which became final during the last few weeks of shooting *Days of Thunder*. Nicole was officially recognised as his new girlfriend when she accompanied him to the 1990 Academy Awards, where he had been nominated for Best Actor for his role in *Born on the Fourth of July*.

When shooting was completed in April, Nicole crossed the continent with Cruise and moved into his house in the exclusive Pacific Palisades area near Los Angeles. The last thing she had expected to happen on her first film in America was that she would fall in love – and accept a proposal of marriage.

I was footloose, ambitious for my career, not at all willing to be tied down in my private life. But after being with Tom for a while, the idea just overwhelmed me. I thought, "God, he's the person I really do want to be with for the rest of my life." God knows we didn't plan it. It just happened.

As a dutiful daughter, Nicole took her young man home to meet her parents. It was Cruise's first trip to Australia

and he fell in love with the place. Janelle had visited the *Days of Thunder* set in Daytona in February and decided that she needed to know more about the handsome young man who was clearly besotted with her daughter. Heading to a local cinema, she found herself in tears at Cruise's performance in *Born on the Fourth of July*. When they heard that Nicole intended to marry Cruise, Janelle admits that they were rather disconcerted until they got to know him, when they shared their daughter's happiness.

While she was in Australia, Nicole filmed a cameo for John Duigan's latest movie, *Flirting* – the last time that she could get away with playing a schoolgirl. Portraying a head prefect with secrets really appealed to Nicole, whose days of illicit smoking and port-drinking at school must have seemed an eternity ago.

Returning to America, Cruise and Kidman tried to keep a low profile. Despite that, stories started to spread of their engagement before Cruise proposed. Then, when they were actually preparing for the wedding, the word on the street was that the romance was over and they were about to go their separate ways.

What really hurts is when the stories are totally untrue. Basically, if someone asks me a question, I answer it. I don't have any secrets, nothing deep and dark that I want to hide. Really in the long run, everyone knows just about all there is to know about me anyway. If people want to do a real investigation into my life, they can. I really don't have any secrets, and I try to answer questions truthfully and honestly.

It was a harsh introduction for Nicole to the world of American tabloid journalism.

BILLY BATHGATE

N ICOLE KIDMAN and Tom Cruise were married on 24 December 1990 at Telluride, Colorado, in a "cute little house we had rented." Both Tom and Nicole wanted a traditional wedding, and that was certainly what they had. Nicole wore her 1930s brocaded dress from the Amsterdam flea market and made sure she included something old, new, borrowed and blue. "It was everything that we hoped, really beautiful," Nicole gushed four months later.

Reportedly, a helicopter chartered by salacious American tabloid the *National*

Enquirer was unable to locate the event. The only witnesses were the bride and groom's family, and some close friends including Dustin Hoffman and his wife. Hoffman had been Cruise's co-star in *Rain Man* and had shared a table on the previous Oscar night with Tom and Nicole on their first public outing together.

He was also Nicole's co-star in *Billy Bathgate*, her next American film. Nicole had unsuccessfully auditioned for a role in *Ghost*, and was looking for a part that would allow her to show more facets of her acting. *Billy Bathgate*

ABOVE: The Gangs of Chicago: The cast of *Billy Bathgate*.

seemed to fit the bill.

Directed by Robert Benton, who was responsible for *Kramer vs Kramer*, Hoffman played the 1920s gangster Dutch Schultz, to whom the title character was apprenticed. Nicole was his rather unusual moll: mysterious socialite Drew Preston, who liked to date gangsters for kicks. Once again, Nicole was playing 'the girl friend, but at least this time it was opposite a highly renowned actor in a far more interesting part.

Billy Bathgate was based on the bestselling novel by E L Doctorow and there were high expectations of it. Once again, *Dead Calm* played a part in Nicole's career – Robert Benton had heard about Nicole's performance and, once he'd watched her take on Billy Zane, he knew she could hold her own against the stellar cast he was putting together. Benton was convinced that he was looking at a major American movie star of the future.

And therein, possibly, lay a problem. For Nicole had a quite definite Australian twang to her voice. Nowadays audiences have become so used to hearing Nicole as an American that when she makes a live appearance as herself it seems somehow 'wrong' to hear her natural voice. However in 1990, she was still known as an Australian – and one whose last role had been made Australian during pre-production once she was cast.

Benton knew that he wanted Nicole for the role, but she had to be an American. She was cast on condition that she learned to speak without a hint of an Australian accent. Like Cruise and the producers of *Days of Thunder*, Benton didn't have a problem with the height difference between Kidman and Hoffman: as Nicole commented wryly, "My size didn't

keep me from getting this great part, but my Australian accent almost did me in."

On *Dead Calm* Nicole learned to walk like an older woman; on *Billy Bathgate* she learned to speak American. In two weeks. Benton supplied Nicole with the name of a voice coach and Nicole focused all her attention on it for two weeks. When it came to the shooting, Benton was absolutely astounded by the transformation.

I had serious doubts that Nicole could entirely drop her Aussie accent in such a short time. She had to be convincingly Park Avenue. But she was phenomenal. Her American accent was perfect. After a long day of shooting, though, she'd revert right back and speak in her natural Australian accent, and the crew were amazed. They asked me, "Why does Nicole talk like an Aussie? Is it some kind of joke?"

The acid test came when she had an official meeting with Hoffman, who was similarly amazed when he couldn't "hear any Sydney" in her voice. Benton and Hoffman were delighted with what Nicole had achieved and were similarly blown away by the quality of her performance. In interviews shortly after the film opened, both men were praising her to the skies, with Benton saying that "Her role was very difficult and challenging, but her performance was utterly flawless. There isn't a single moment that I would change." Hoffman added that "Her instincts are unerring. There's behaviour and then there's acting. You can't act behaviour. You can't act a sense of humour if you don't have one."

Once again, Nicole was determined

to learn as much as she could during the shoot. If she had problems over her motivations in her scene, she would ask Hoffman's advice – but the veteran actor simply advised her to follow her instincts. Nicole would later comment that working with Hoffman was better than three years of drama training.

Nicole also maintained her sense of fun during what at times was a tough shoot, particularly when the film started going over-budget. A lot of the trauma went over her head; she was so high on the excitement of working on the film that she forgot that, at the end of the day, the film's success would be judged not by its artistic merits but by the (disappointing, as it turned out) box-office receipts. There was still an element of the 'arthouse' film actor in Nicole; she wanted her projects to be judged on what people saw, not how many people came to see it.

On one occasion, in the middle of a scene with Hoffman, Nicole suddenly started to bark at him like a dog, just to tease him. According to Tom Cruise, who was a regular visitor to the set, Hoffman was just a little bit scared of this Australian 'kook'.

It seems odd, then, that it was around this time that rumours started to circulate about Nicole Kidman – that she was an ice maiden, that she was humourless and that, because she was Mrs Tom Cruise, somehow she thought she was better than everyone else. Maybe it was jealousy; after all, Cruise was briefly one of the most eligible bachelors in America. Maybe it was simply xenophobia. The American press are quite capable of slating someone simply because they're not American, conveniently forgetting that

ABOVE: With Dustin Hoffman on location for *Billy Bathgate*.

the vast majority of all Americans are descended from immigrants.

Certainly those who worked on *Billy Bathgate* wanted to work with her again. During shooting, Hoffman approached Benton suggesting strongly that the three of them should make another movie soon, and Benton recalls there being a really happy family atmosphere on the movie.

But unfortunately, the paying public didn't agree. The film grossed less than $16m in America and was judged to be a flop. It wasn't another *Die Hard*, so Bruce Willis' fans were disappointed; it wasn't another *Days of Thunder*. The critics didn't like it either. Roger Ebert dismissed Hoffman's performance as "dispensable" and Nicole as "a character cobbled together from old Scott Fitzgerald stories – we never feel her as real." It was the first major period piece that Nicole had done on film, but by no means her last.

Nicole wasn't that worried about the future. Talking to *Australian Women's Weekly* a few weeks after her wedding, she revealed:

You know, you worry you'll never get another acting job, you worry it's all going to end. At one point, I found it hard to enjoy my success. But then I decided I had to re-evaluate everything. I thought, "Hold on a minute, I don't want to live like this." I didn't like the feeling that now I was successful it could all be taken away. So I have more faith now. More faith in myself and my ability.

The cause of her change of attitude? The support system that she had found in her marriage to Tom Cruise. She was very much in love with him and really believed that she had found the person with whom she would spend the rest of her life.

Not that she was going to be changing her name any time soon. She had made her name as Nicole Kidman and had no intention of becoming Nicole Cruise just to satisfy outdated prejudices. She was hoping to have babies at some point, although she recognised that she was still only 23 and just married. She wanted to do everything – comedy, romance, drama. "Wherever the good roles are, that's where I want to be," she said pointedly.

From the start, Cruise and Kidman laid down rules to ensure that their marriage had a good chance of surviving. Cruise came from a broken home and had made a disastrous first marriage; Kidman's parents were together, despite the occasional short separation and blazing row. Nicole insisted that Cruise still ask her out for dates; as she pointed out, why should either of them just assume anything or take the other person for granted? They agreed that they would not be separated for any length of time, which became adjusted when they adopted their two children to mean that one of them would look after the children while the other worked.

Both Cruise and Kidman were essentially private people, and would much rather spend time with each other than living it up in the latest Hollywood nightclub. They both had a wanderlust; "We both have gypsy blood in our veins," Nicole joked. They shared an interest in exotic sports – scuba diving and horseback - riding at first, but soon they were learning the excitement of skydiving from an aeroplane.

All that was missing was a major role for Nicole. The solution? *Far and Away.*

FAR AND AWAY

WITH the benefit of hindsight, it might not have been the best move that Mr and Mrs Cruise could have made, if part of the intention was to ensure the continuation of Nicole Kidman's film career. While *Far and Away* entranced many of those who went to see it, it was very definitely a movie which focused on the Cruises and helped to reinforce the 'TomandNicole' image that was already beginning to infuriate Nicole.

When *Far and Away* was announced, initially as *Irish Story* and then as *Distant Shores*, it sounded like a wonderful idea. Tom and Nicole would play Joseph and Shannon, feisty Irish immigrants to America, the action following them from their roots in Southern Ireland, across the Atlantic to their eventual home in the States. Along the way, there would be plenty of opportunity for humour, drama and romance, as well as a chance for Cruise to display his muscles in assorted bare-knuckle fights. The couple, who were still behaving like newlyweds, could mix their personal and business lives, keeping their vows not to spend anything longer than two weeks apart.

Far and Away boasted a script by Bob Dolman from a story by Dolman and the film's director, Ron Howard; both men had previously worked together in 1988 on *Willow*. Although *Far and Away* was removed from the earlier film's fantasy background, it contained enough whimsy and Irish cliché to sink it. Its major plus point was that it was the first film shot in 70mm for many years, which meant that at least the Oklahoma countryside looked

wonderful on the big screen.

Cruise and Kidman enjoyed working on the film, and Ron Howard was able to play on Nicole's sense of humour when he needed a particular reaction

ABOVE: Shannon Christie – ready for the New World in *Far and Away.*

shot from her. When Shannon lifts a bowl that's been covering Joseph's crotch, Howard wanted something rather more than he was getting from Nicole. Without letting her know, he told Cruise to remove his underwear before the next take. He duly did – and Nicole's genuine reaction is enshrined on celluloid.

A less pleasant occurrence added weight to rumours of the amount of control Cruise and Kidman were demanding over their private lives. A photo of them with the whole crew was allegedly 'killed' on their

ABOVE: Shannon Christie and Joseph Donnelly (Tom Cruise) ponder their future in *Far and Away*.

instructions, leaving a large number of people disappointed not to have a memento of their time working with a couple rapidly becoming regarded as Hollywood royalty.

Nicole's natural Australian openness was now being rapidly eroded by the persistent demands of the tabloid press. Stories continually circulated that she and Cruise had a sham marriage because Cruise was homosexual, or that their membership of the Church of Scientology meant that they did not have a 'proper' marriage. Unsurprisingly, Nicole became less open with the press and, as she did so, the stories began to get more and more vicious.

Ron Howard was very impressed with his female lead and, after shooting had been completed, he was heard to refer to her as "another Katharine Hepburn". He also recognised something that was becoming increasingly clear to Kidman herself – she was being regarded as little more than the eye candy on Tom Cruise's arm, only cast because of who she was married to rather than for her own talents. Looking back in 1998, he commented:

> It pissed me off when people were dismissive of Nicole because she was married to Tom. She handled it so beautifully. I was so frustrated for her. But talent will out...

Film roles didn't seem to be coming Nicole's way, and she realised that she had been naïve to imagine that she would be able to do "tons of work" without anyone ever judging her. It simply wasn't the case. It seemed as if she would forever be judged as Mrs Tom Cruise. It was the downside of her marriage, although Nicole pointed out the upside when she said that "I get to go to bed with Tom Cruise. Every night."

Nicole appeared in two movies released in 1993 – *Malice* with Alec Baldwin and *My Life* with Michael Keaton. Neither film really gave her a chance to showcase her talents, although her display of ferocity in *Malice* gave fuel to those who believed she was a bitch in real life. Anyone who could believably deliver a description of a blind little boy as "a little fucking troll who deserves to be put out of his misery for fucking up my life" couldn't possibly be the sweet, fun-loving woman that Cruise was constantly praising in interviews.

Nicole balanced *Malice* with her performance as the pregnant wife of a man dying of lung cancer in *My Life*, which gave her a chance to work with *Ghost*'s writer, Bruce Joel Rubin, on his directorial debut. However, as *Rolling Stone*'s reviewer pointed out, "Kidman looks lovely, as usual, but her chief function is to assist reconciliation between Bob and his Ukrainian parents, played by Michael Constantine and Rebecca Schull, who resent him for changing his name from Ivanovich." This wasn't what Nicole Kidman came to America to do.

But then it seemed as if the well had run dry. Nicole went through a period where she didn't get any work for a year. She even contemplated returning to Australia, but her marriage was more important to her – and Cruise's career was most definitely in America. By this time, there were other considerations as well. In December 1992, a young baby girl was born who would soon be adopted into the Cruise-Kidman household as Isabella.

Her adoptive parents became almost paranoid in their attempts to keep her out of the limelight. Even Isabella's natural mother had no idea who they were. No one was allowed to photograph her – with one unfortunate exception, which saw Tom and Nicole defending their daughter's rights in the Australian courts.

ABOVE: Arriving at the premiere for *Far and Away* in May 1992.

On 13 February 1993, the Cruises held a small family gathering at their apartment to celebrate Isabella's adoption, and Cruise's executive assistant was asked to take photos of the new family. The film was taken for processing by another trusted employee, who waited while they were developed and printed, then returned the photos and negatives to Tom and Nicole. But somehow, copies managed to get out. On 18 March, the Cruises learned that the photos of Isabella were about to be published by *New Idea* magazine. Desperate to protect her privacy, they tried to get the magazine to forget the idea, but when they couldn't get an acceptable answer, they had to take out an injunction. Their grounds were that either the photos had been stolen or taken without their consent; that their fans might think that they were trying to exploit their daughter, so publication would be defaming them; and that they owned the copyright in the photos.

Unfortunately, while the judge had every sympathy for the Cruises' desire to protect Isabella, he was unable to grant them the injunction; Australia simply didn't have the legal framework to give them a general right of privacy. That was it as far as the Cruises were

ABOVE:
Tracy Kennsinger:
uncertain where the
threat really lies
in *Malice.*

TOP RIGHT:
Gail and Bob Jones
(Michael Keaton)
making every
moment count
in *My Life.*

concerned – their children became off limits. When they adopted African-American Connor in 1995, any questions regarding his mixed heritage and ethnic background were completely out of order, and the rare mentions of his race in interviews only came about when Nicole experienced racial tensions while out in the street with her son.

Neither Tom or Nicole have ever felt it right to discuss the reasons why they chose to adopt first Isabella and then Connor, not wanting their children to find out why from the pages of a book or a magazine. Initially, Nicole had been very clear in interviews that she wanted to bear Cruise's children. The adoptions gave credence to those who were claiming that Cruise was sterile, and also fuelled the fire of those who believed Cruise was gay. After trying to ignore the stories, Nicole eventually used an interview in the highly regarded American journal *Entertainment Weekly* to put the record straight.

Honestly, wholeheartedly, looking you straight in the eye – it's not true. It's utterly ridiculous, a total rumour. I suppose because I'm married to somebody very famous, our love life is under great speculation by many, many people at their dinner tables every night. But it gets invasive. Both of us are private people. We don't feel comfortable discussing what we do in bed at midnight – even though it is pretty damn good. Look, Tom and I are heterosexual, we're together, we're in love. It's weird even to have to answer that question.

Nicole Kidman's personal life had just been changed dramatically – and her professional life was about to receive an equally dramatic reassessment when Jane Campion reappeared in Nicole's life.

CHANGING THE IMAGE

N EW ZEALAND-born director Jane Campion had come a long way in the 11 years since she wanted Nicole to take part in her student film at the Australian School of Film and Television. At the time she felt that Nicole stood out because of her incredible passion and facility for making things seem immediate and real, and, when her plans were thwarted, she encouraged Nicole's acting dreams by hoping that one day she would direct Nicole in a classic.

Every film Campion directed won awards – even her very first short film, *Peel*, won the Palme d'Or at Cannes – and she was the very first woman to win the Best Film Palme d'Or for her feature, *The Piano*, which also netted her an Academy Award for Best Screenplay. All her films took risks with their subject matter and style. *A Girl's Own Story* dealt with marital

ABOVE:
A rare glimpse of
Connor Cruise, out
with his parents.

crisis, incest, child abuse and teenage confusion and ended with its young heroines singing a song directly to camera. *The Piano*, starring Holly Hunter, had amazed and delighted audiences around the world with its insight and beautiful imagery.

She and Nicole had kept in touch, and their paths had crossed on a few occasions. Despite discussions between them, though, none of Campion's projects seemed right for Nicole until

ABOVE: With *The Portrait of A Lady* director Jane Campion at the Tropicana Film Festval in Sydney.

Campion decided early in 1993 that she wanted to start work on a version of one of her favourite novels, Henry James' *The Portrait of a Lady*. However, by the time that she and Nicole began to discuss the lead role, it seemed that the British partnership of Merchant Ivory were thinking about doing a film version of their own. Nicole encouraged her longtime friend to stick with the project; after all, there was nothing stopping both companies working on the same material.

Nicole loved the thought of playing Isabel, the heroine. She had read James' novel when she was 17 and, as she became increasingly mature, she began to understand the complexities of the female psyche James was

investigating. The part of Isabel seemed tailor-made for her.

Henry James wrote with the character of Isabel that pain and suffering can teach you and take you places, and give you understanding about how there are those situations in life and how you deal with them. At 17 it didn't mean much to me. It was more like you're hoping for a good mark, but it didn't hit me as it did when I was 22. Obviously that was because great literature speaks to you when you yourself have experienced things which make it accessible to you. At that stage when I read about Isabel I felt like I was reading things about myself. Her reactions were different and unpredictable, but I could understand them; it's almost like grasping different concepts on how to deal with things. It's like being transported in a way, which is very exciting.

When they started discussing the project, Campion thought Nicole was a good fit for the part, but by the time she had been able to pull the finance together, she began to have second thoughts. The strengths that she had seen in Nicole's acting in her Australian work seemed to have been diminished by her, frankly, one-dimensional roles in Hollywood.

In the time that Nicole was in Hollywood, she'd made quite a few films I didn't think suited her, and I don't think she felt suited her either. I started to feel unconfident about it, and felt the only way for it to work for me was if we did a couple of days' audition. Which is a terrible thing to tell someone when you basically said, "Oh you can have the part."

Unsurprisingly, Nicole was devastated by this rejection from someone who had been such a strong influence on her decision to go into acting in the first place. She wasn't going to take it lying down, and Campion recalls a number of difficult and confrontational telephone calls in which she began to see the spirit of Isabel shining through once more. Nicole revealed to Campion that she too wasn't pleased with some of the work she had been doing – Campion claimed in a later interview that Nicole actually hated the material – and that she was on the verge of giving up acting. Nicole was desperate to work on something that she could believe in.

While Nicole was battling for the role, Tom Cruise tried to be supportive, but the couple resigned themselves to the fact that Nicole would lose any chance of working on the project if that's what the director wanted. But that wasn't the case. Campion knew that the spirited Australian girl she had first encountered was still a fundamental part of Nicole, and was willing to give her every opportunity to prove herself. They spent a full two days together, improvising scenes, rehearsing material from a draft of the script, relaxing together and even indulging in a spot of go-go dancing. Campion warned Nicole that she wouldn't give her an immediate answer, and that there would probably be a week's gap before she let her know the outcome.

It was positive. Campion called Nicole at home and told her that she was "her Isabel" – and Nicole broke down in tears. In *The Portrait of a Lady*, Isabel's spirit is broken down by her circumstances, and then rebuilt. Nicole recognised that Campion had put her

through much the same process.

But *The Portrait of a Lady* didn't actually go into production for another two years. Once Jane Campion had finished adapting the 650-page novel for the screen, she suffered a personal tragedy when her first child died shortly after birth. Plans for the filming were unsurprisingly put on hold.

Nicole took the opportunity to make some changes. She knew that she had to change the perception of her as 'Mrs Tom Cruise', playing roles which were simply 'filler'. Looking back in March 1996, she pointed out some home truths to *Juice* magazine:

> People think, "Oh you chose to do something like *Malice* or *My Life*," but that's really not true. That's all you have to choose from. People think you were turning down *Thelma & Louise* for *Malice*. And that's just not the case. You don't have those options. They go to Jodie Foster and Michelle Pfeiffer and all those girls.

Nicole was re-evaluating why she wanted to be an actor. For her, acting was always about shaking herself up and not doing the things she knew she could do. She wanted to go after the unknown. She wanted roles like Isabel Archer, not characters like *Malice*'s Tracy Kennsinger or *My Life*'s Gail Jones: she just didn't find them complex or interesting.

> I would credit Jane with a lot of changes in me, and my ability to be able to say no to things and to be able to stand up for myself and go, "I know what I want to do: I want to do this, and I'm going to hang out until something like that comes along."

ABOVE: Mrs Tom Cruise attending a promotional event for her husband's John Grisham thriller *The Firm*.

She did not want to be known just as Mrs Tom Cruise. She knew that she had a strong idea of who she was but, because Cruise's films were making box-office fortunes, all eyes in the industry were on him. She felt that she was 'just the wife'. She wasn't blaming Cruise for the fact that, at parties, all eyes were directed at him – but it was beginning to hurt. The last thing anyone expected her to do was to go onto popular comedy show *Saturday Night Live* and use her monologue as a fake attack on Tom Cruise – but that's what she did.

Nor did anyone expect her to go back to school: but she did that too. The Actors' Studio in New York is renowned worldwide for its teaching of The Method, which helps an actor get in tune with the character he or she is playing by coming to understand and live the life that character would lead. And for an actor like Nicole Kidman, whose believable reactions had been spotted by John Duigan half her lifetime earlier, it was like coming home. It changed her whole life and made her realise the falseness of the pursuit of the Almighty Dollar. So what if her husband's 1993 movie *The Firm* grossed $262.3m worldwide against a $42m budget? She would look for films like the ones she had been seeking when she began her career in Australia – with parts and characters that attracted her, that challenged her. No more characters like those in *Malice* and *My Life*. She needed a part to die for – and Suzanne Stone Moretto fit the bill rather nicely...

TO DIE FOR

THE producers wanted Meg Ryan for the part. They got Nicole Kidman.

After the rapturous reception that *To Die For* gained at the Cannes Film Festival in 1995, they knew that they had got the better part of the deal. And that was before it started getting nominations and awards from film festivals and auspicious bodies such as BAFTA and the Golden Globe judges.

Not everyone around Nicole Kidman wanted her to get the part. *To Die For* was an independent movie, not part of the studio system, so it wouldn't have the backing that a major movie would have. And they warned her that the public have a problem with differentiating between the parts someone plays on screen and who they really are. And Suzanne Stone Moretto was definitely not someone you'd want to cuddle up with or have as your best girlfriend. She looked after one person in her life – Suzanne Stone Moretto.

Nicole's friends were right in a sense, since the rumours about her were magnified by her performance – no matter how often she pointed out to critics that that's what acting is all about. But the effect that working on *To Die For* and *The Portrait of a Lady* had on her career is inestimable. Both films showed, once and for all, that Nicole Kidman could act, that the promise she had showed in *Dead Calm* hadn't been squandered in Hollywood – that she wasn't just fit to play what Jane Campion had derisively called "handbags".

Nicole went after the part of Suzanne once she had read the script and learned that Meg Ryan had bowed out. Suzanne is a greedy, grasping small-town girl who dreams of becoming a famous TV personality – one key scene shows her watching her own image on a video when she's only a small girl. She talks her way into a job as a weather girl on the local cable station

ABOVE: The sort of supply teacher every teenager dreams of: Suzanne Stone Moretto in *To Die For*.

and starts to make a name for herself. But when her 'local boy' husband wants her to pack up the job and help him with his bar, she seduces three teenagers both morally and physically and persuades them to kill him.

Nicole found the role very funny, and rather ironic, given her own situation.

> I saw the burnout in playing a character who's obsessed with celebrity. It was just one of those parts which you read and go "Wow!"

She also knew that it wasn't exactly the sort of role that she was well known for in America. While she had appeared in some comedies in Australia, notably the bittersweet *Emerald City*, her work Stateside had all been in dramatic roles. She knew that, once again, people's perceptions of her would work against her but, just as Suzanne wanted fame, so Nicole wanted Suzanne. The film was being directed by Gus Van Sant, at that time

ABOVE: Suzanne and canine friend refusing to answer questions after her husband's murder in *To Die For.*

highly regarded for his work on *Drugstore Cowboy* and *My Private Idaho*. Nicole couldn't see she had anything to lose by making direct contact; he might not be willing to cast her, but at least by ringing him she had the chance to

put her case. After all, that seemed to have done the trick with Jane Campion.

When Van Sant answered the phone, Nicole made it clear to him that she believed she was destined to play Suzanne. Van Sant initially thought that it was a ploy, but the hour-long conversation that followed persuaded him that maybe it was the truth. Nicole needed someone to give her the opportunity to appear in an American film and demonstrate the other facets to her acting ability. By the end of the conversation, not only had he cast her but he believed that it really might have been predestined after all. After some considerable discussion, the film's producers eventually came round to Van Sant's way of thinking. They were working with someone who had a reputation for bucking the system and approaching things in a way that others wouldn't – so maybe he was right on this occasion.

This was the first opportunity for Nicole to put into practice the lessons she had learned at the Actors' Studio. Her aim was simple – she wanted to make Suzanne more complex than "just some total fucked-up bitch." She was playing a small-town American woman, so in the pre-production period, while the producers were getting the finances together, she spent three months "studying American women". Then, once she felt she had a handle on how a small-town American woman might think and move, she and Cruise booked themselves into a small motor inn in the California town of Santa Barbara, locked the door and switched on the TV. There was one simple rule – no matter how bad, how trashy, how unutterably terrible what they saw on screen was, they didn't switch the TV off. The effects stayed with Nicole for some time.

LEFT:
The happy couple:
Tom and Nicole
enjoying each
other's company.

I found out that TV deadens you, and it's hypnotic. I would get involved in the talk shows, yelling back at the screen. One of the shows had these two who were obsessed with the same serial killer. It ended up with one clobbering the other and they had to be removed from the stage! Outrageous!

To Die For's producers struggled to raise the $11m budget needed for the film, and in the end the decision was made to shoot north of the border in the eastern Canadian city of Toronto. Although home to a number of major landmarks, including the CN Tower, Toronto's skyline is sufficiently similar to New York's to have stood in for the city on numerous occasions. Also, the nearby Ontario countryside is comparatively only a hop, skip and a jump from its counterpart the other side of the St Lawrence river in the northern United States. By shooting in Canada, the producers also raised money from the country's tax incentives and saved themselves a fortune.

When she filmed *Billy Bathgate*, Nicole played a convincing American lady on screen but reverted to her natural accent off camera. For *To Die For*, she went one stage further and spoke in her American accent from the minute she started rehearsing to the minute she finished the movie. She didn't take her Method acting to ridiculous levels – she didn't insist on being called Suzanne off-camera, for example – but she maintained the poise and accent. She found that she perceived things more intensely, and it helped her maintain the very high energy level that Suzanne required. She even learned to edit film so that she could work on the editing of the film-within-a-film, just as Suzanne did.

She also ensured that one other distraction wasn't around. Tom Cruise found himself not simply unwelcome on set, but actually told not to come a-calling. It was his turn to look after Isabella, so he took the opportunity to practise his flying in and around Toronto, as he was working for his pilot's licence. Nicole knew she'd find it too hard to create a character with someone who knew her so well watching from behind the camera.

Gus Van Sant joined the ranks of directors who enjoyed working with Nicole Kidman, admiring the notebook she kept, with details of exercises to use in preparation for every scene:

> She was a really great ally on set. We never had disagreements. We just mostly had fun. It surprised me how much I was laughing.

The film inspired an increase in interest in Nicole from the world's press. There were still reports about her and Tom Cruise's private lives,

one claiming that she and Cruise had ordered four chicken potpies from the Mulholland Drive Café to be delivered to their hotel room – and Nicole doesn't even like chicken. But now, serious journalists were asking her about the films that she was doing, not what Tom Cruise was like in bed.

Nicole was delighted with the reaction to the film; she received some of the best reviews she'd ever had. Roger Ebert proclaimed that she was "superb at making Suzanne into someone who is not only stupid, vain and egomaniacal (we've seen that before) but also vulnerably human. She represents, on a large scale, feelings we have all had in smaller and sneakier ways. She simply lacks skill in concealing them." *Rolling Stone* noted that she looked "like an erotic ice cream sundae in her pastel suits, teddies and fuck-me pumps ... She struts her stuff – bidda-bim-bidda-boom – with enough come-on carnality to singe the screen." It didn't surprise Nicole that the film was the hit of the 1995 Cannes Film Festival, or that Cruise would be calling their three-year-old daughter excitedly on the night of the Golden Globes to tell her that "Mommy's won! Mommy's won!"

Her next choice of movie surprised everyone – but then, that's what Nicole wanted to do. She'd had enough of being predictable. She'd already worked with Michael Keaton on one of his first movies after hanging up Batman's cape. Now she was cast as Dr Chase Meridien in the Caped Crusader debut of Keaton's successor Val Kilmer: *Batman Forever*. It took her into Cruise's territory in terms of the sheer size of the film – and this time, she was cast because of who she was, not because of who she had married.

BELOW:
Cuddling up to
the Caped Crusader
(Val Kilmer) in
the promotional
artwork for
Batman Returns.

BATMAN FOREVER

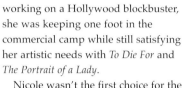

I N mid-1995, Jane Campion was gearing up to begin filming *The Portrait of a Lady* when she discovered Nicole's choice of film to precede it. Jane was surprised, but it was clear that there was method in Kidman's seeming madness. By working on a Hollywood blockbuster, she was keeping one foot in the commercial camp while still satisfying her artistic needs with *To Die For* and *The Portrait of a Lady*.

Nicole wasn't the first choice for the Bat-hungry Dr Chase Meridien, whose interest in the Dark Knight goes well beyond the purely professional – until she meets the even more psychiatrically challenged Bruce Wayne and gets caught up in his battle with The Riddler and Two-Face. When it looked as if Michael Keaton might complete a trilogy of films as Batman, Rene Russo, who had recently starred as Mel Gibson's love interest in *Lethal Weapon 3*, was the main contender. However, as filming approached and Keaton dropped out to be replaced by Val Kilmer, 'scheduling conflicts' became clear and Russo also dropped out. There were rumours that Sandra Bullock, hot from her breakthrough role as Annie in *Speed*, was top of the list. But one man had had his eye on Nicole for some time.

Director Joel Schumacher was keen to make his mark on the series as he was stepping into the shoes of Tim Burton, whose iconic imagery had established Batman as something rather more than the two-dimensional comic book rip-off that most superhero films had become. When pressed about why he cast Nicole, he protested:

Nicole is a great character actress with the body and face of a movie star ... I know, I know, she doesn't look anything like a criminal psychiatrist, but it's my Gotham City and I can do what I want. I've had

my eye on Nicole since *Dead Calm*. You meet a lot of beautiful people in this business, but there's something almost luminous about her. I wish I had a clause in my contract that said Nicole Kidman had to be in every one of my movies.

Describing Nicole some time after filming *Batman Forever*, Schumacher called her an obsessive-compulsive – and it's a fair description of the way in which Nicole approaches her movie roles. If she was going to play a criminal psychiatrist in anything other than a *Batman* movie, she would probably have read texts by FBI profilers like John Douglas. But this wasn't reality – this was a hyper-reality where schizophrenic former District Attorneys have their faces literally divided in two, and overlooked scientists invent machines that can extract brain power from the local population. Instead, Jim Carrey, who was cast as The Riddler, gave her some far more useful reading material – some of the plethora of graphic novels created about the Batman. Nicole found them "amazing, with the weird angles and strange sort of writing. There are some incredibly strong images."

Nicole enjoyed the outlandish elements of the role. Chase Meridien is constantly trying to seduce Batman. She wears black slinky dresses, has perfect hair, perfect red lips and talks in a deep husky voice. Even after she and Bruce Wayne have been attacked by Two Face's henchmen, there's hardly a hair out of place. The only time she seems at all exerted is when she's practising her kickboxing – a skill Nicole acquired courtesy of her husband, whose only stipulation, she joked, was that she didn't use it on him.

From all accounts, *Batman Forever* wasn't the easiest of films to shoot but it was a major success financially, setting the record for an opening weekend at the box-office. Critically, despite Jonathan Ross' comment that it was "one of the greatest movies ever made", it certainly didn't make any major waves. It did, however, achieve one of Nicole's aims. Once again people were talking about her, not her husband.

While publicising the release of the two movies (*To Die For* didn't actually get a general release until September 1995, three months after *Batman Forever* dominated screens worldwide), Nicole opened up more about her private life. It was clear that six years after her audition for *Days of Thunder*, she was still as head over heels in love with Tom Cruise as she had been on the day they wed.

The children were still off-limits as far as the press were concerned – even if Isabella herself, or Bella as she was known, had less compunction about chatting to them, proudly announcing that she was special because she was adopted – but Nicole was as effusive about Tom as she'd been in interviews conducted only months after the wedding.

Our relationship is hard work. It's not some sort of fairytale. You have to keep working at it but, luckily, it's also based on a thing where I go, "God, I just love being with this person." With Tom, I always loved his sense of humour ... More than anything, that's the thing that ties us together: any situation, no matter what happens, no matter what they write about us, we can laugh. And if you can have that as a couple, you have a lifelong friendship. Of all the people in the world, he's the one that makes me say, "That's who I want to be with."

Having two young children put a strain on the Cruises, no matter how many nannies and support staff they had. Nicole wanted to give her children as emotionally normal an upbringing as she could, and if that meant she was sitting up all night with them and then having to get up for a 6.00 am call the next day, she just hoped that the make-up team could repair the damage.

She also made sure that she and her husband had quality time together. She would grin wickedly when describing the Saturday evenings when she and Tom would book a hotel room and go off to stay the night together, just the two of them. She made it clear to Cruise when they married that she wasn't prepared to sit inside, giving up the things she loved doing, just because they were famous. However, even when they put baseball caps and sunglasses on and ventured out to the

movies or to the park with their children, chances were that someone would recognise them. But Nicole accepted that it came with the territory. Giving an autograph wasn't necessarily the end of the world.

I don't think it's right to sit around and say, "I don't like being famous." I find that indulgent. You've got to be willing to sign autographs and chat with people or you'll be miserable. People who fight it end up flipping out. It's one of the things my husband has done really well. He's been famous for well over a decade, and he's totally sane...

As she prepared for the demanding shoot on *The Portrait of a Lady*, Nicole relished the time the family spent in London, which was starting to become a regular stopping-off place for them. Whether she was playing pool in a backstreet Chelsea pub against the locals or having a picnic in Hyde Park, Nicole Kidman was enjoying life.

RIGHT:
Tom and Nicole at the premiere of Batman Forever.

THE PORTRAIT OF A LADY

I F Jane Campion had had her way originally, *The Portrait of a Lady* would probably have starred Nicole Kidman in her first stage performance for five years. When she was making her plans in 1993,

Campion's first thought had been that it would work better in a theatrical environment. But when she learned of Merchant Ivory's proposed version, she knew that she ought to get her visualisation committed to film

BELOW:
Isabel Archer realises that life doesn't always go to plan in *The Portrait of A Lady.*

as soon as possible.

That didn't mean everything went straight in front of the cameras once Campion had her script and finance arranged by mid-1995. In order to get the performances she required, Campion insisted on a lengthy rehearsal and discussion period before one foot of film was shot. So, while Nicole was spending her evenings watching Cruise give a "*Color of Money* performance" (ie, playing pool brilliantly) at the Chelsea pub, her days were spent discussing and 'workshopping', as well as listening to a lot of music recorded by blues legend Nina Simone.

The two-day audition that Campion had made Nicole undergo in Los Angeles back in 1993 certainly helped build trust between director and actor. Nicole knew that she had her director's backing and confidence, while Campion could be certain that Nicole was going into the project aware of her expectations and demands. With hindsight, Nicole was glad she had gone through that at-the-time morale-sapping experience, since she knew that she had won the role on a fair basis.

BELOW:
An atmospheric
Portrait of A Lady.

Although Campion didn't expect her actors to rewrite the script during the rehearsal process, she would nevertheless go away from the discussions and work with writer Laura Jones in the light of what she had learned. The cast went through a lot of improvisations, while Campion delved into their psyches to learn what made them tick – so she knew what buttons to press at which time during the filming process.

There are scenes in the film where I'm talking and I sniff my shoes or put a candlestick on my head: that came out during improvisation when [Jane Campion] said, "Just do

something" – that'd be one of, say, 20 things I tried, and then she'd choose one. You feel with her like you're making a student film, which I love: it's as if she doesn't know the rules, as if she's shocked by the way other people make films. That's why she likes this huge rehearsal process: one of her greatest attributes is her perceptiveness. She's able to find things in human behaviour not many people pay attention to, able to notice things about certain actors and put them on film. You talk a lot ... a lot of it just sitting around drinking coffee and smoking cigarettes.

Before rehearsals began, Nicole started her homework in her usual way, re-reading James' novel and then studying the many articles and treatises that had been written about Isabel's character. Unfortunately, they weren't a great deal of help, as each writer had their own perception of Isabel Archer and they were often contradictory. Nicole appealed to Campion for help and the New Zealander's reaction was blunt. "Burn them – this has to be personal," she told Nicole, and advised her to wait for the rehearsal period.

The key to Isabel that Campion and Nicole discovered was that she was someone who, when she was younger, simply didn't have a sense of humour. For someone so in love with life as Nicole, who could find humour in most situations, this was a great challenge and one she embraced willingly. Campion's idea of Isabel was that she was serious, intense, without cynicism or wit. She shouldn't have any of "the tricks that women develop to attract men."

Neither woman wanted to make what Campion called "a *Reader's Digest*" version of James' novel – the film needed to explore James' understanding of human perversity while still being a valid cinematic experience. When they removed much of the first third of the novel, which includes a lot of setting-up of the situations that pay off later, they were left with the book's strengths, notably James' dialogue.

The film follows the very independently minded American heiress Isabel as she turns down suitors in London and travels to Tuscany. She eventually marries Gilbert Osmond, a devious aesthete who is concerned primarily with his exquisite self-image. However, she's simply become one more piece for his art collection; he is in fact not interested in her as a person at all. Isabel detests the fact that she's attracted to Osmond, but she can't free herself of that attraction.

We're dealing with the dark side of attraction. Why do you choose the person that is wrong for you, when you should ultimately be searching for the person that's right? Jane and I both have had relationships like that. I find that fascinating, the incredible power one person can have over another. And those relationships can be so amazing too.

By the end of the film, Isabel has realised that Osmond is the wrong person for her, and chooses the love of her dying cousin, Ralph, sharing a last tender moment with him before he passes away.

Nicole was working with a very strong cast, including John Malkovich as Osmond. She admits that she was a little in awe of him when they began filming, although it helped that they were using an old hall in London as a rehearsal room – it took Nicole back to her early days of working in Sydney. When she first met him, she couldn't

believe that she was expected to start work straightaway, wanting a chance to chat and get to know the man she described as "one of the great actors of his generation." But Campion insisted on going straight into an improvisation, and Nicole knew she had to get a grip on herself.

Nicole never wastes an emotion she's experienced, and she used her fascination with Malkovich to help her explore Isabel's fascination with Osmond. By the end of filming, the two actors had become firm friends. That helped, because the shoot itself was tiring, both physically and mentally, particularly once the unit arrived in Italy.

Making *Portrait of a Lady* wasn't about glamour. It was about getting up and there's no hot water in the little villa so you've got to have a cold shower at 5.00 am so that you can be in the make-up chair by 5.30 and you're freezing your tits off in the shower going, "Oh no...!"

The cast didn't finish work at the end of the day and just head out for dinner. The intensity of the shoot stayed with them throughout, slowly but surely exhausting them all. Nicole found that although her everyday life had to go on – she still came home and bathed and fed the children – she felt herself becoming much more sensitive and highly emotional. The discussion process continued throughout filming and, at the end, it was clear that Nicole had felt both challenged and satiated.

I'd wake up and know I had to go to work and deal with all these abusive relationships, and that was weird: it was like Isabel took over my life. As an actor you have to be willing to

ABOVE: Isabel Archer takes the air with Gilbert Osmond (John Malkovich) in *The Portrait of A Lady.*

give up a lot. I don't know whether that's just my self-punishment, but where there are certain films that you don't do that on (like *Batman Forever,* obviously), it did work on *To Die For* or *Portrait,* and it's the same with Kubrick: films that deserve it.

Malkovich and Nicole worked together to help make the film less static than the original novel. The actors wanted to elevate the scenes between Osmond and Isabel, and make them more physical and sexual. In one scene, Isabel is becoming so frustrated at herself that she beats her head against a wall. That wasn't scripted – it just felt natural to Nicole, and she had the bruise on her forehead to prove it next day. But once Campion had seen it, she ended up demanding further takes, since it added so much to Isabel's progression. Nicole didn't want to make Isabel 'cold' – she preferred to show Isabel having emotions, but constantly conflicting ones. Malkovich added in a number of physical movements, including stepping on the hem of Isabel's dress to stop her moving away and slapping her with a glove. "I got slapped by that glove, it must have been about a hundred times, and John really whacked me!" Nicole commented later.

Eventually, for one week, the emotion became too intense, and Nicole knew that she couldn't juggle her home life with the emotions she needed to maintain. Cruise therefore took the children away for a week's holiday.

Not that Nicole and Tom didn't get some time away for themselves. There was no possibility of their sightseeing around the Colosseum and the other tourist spots in Rome without being attacked by fans – even disguises wouldn't have much effect. Nicole knew the city, after filming *Un'Australiana a Roma* there some years earlier, and was determined that her husband wasn't going to miss out. So at 3.00 am, the Cruises climbed over the walls around the Colosseum and had their own private wander around!

Unfortunately, *The Portrait of a Lady* wasn't the success that Campion's previous film, *The Piano,* had been. Although *Entertainment Weekly* praised Nicole for taking a chance on the project for art's sake, others weren't so kind. "Though Campion and writer Laura Jones reprise the highlights of the novel, *Portrait* is woefully free of all but its most banal significances and subtexts. And despite Isabel Archer's protracted sufferings, this picture is oddly un-charged, indistinct and even long-winded," wrote the *Washington Post,* while filmcritic.com pointed out that while *Portrait* "is a fantastic movie to watch, exquisitely crafted and painstakingly detailed, gorgeously photographed and full of style – it is just plain impossible to follow." Hardly words that were going to encourage an audience to flock to the cinemas. The film never had a chance of recouping its budget.

But that was in the future as far as Nicole was concerned. Once the shooting was complete, she needed to take some time off. Her next project promised to be just as gruelling – working with the legendary Stanley Kubrick. If Nicole survived long enough to make it to the start of filming...

THE PEACEMAKER

ALTHOUGH the *Portrait of a Lady* shoot exhausted Nicole emotionally, it didn't prevent her from indulging in her usual pastimes – and, as ever, the more dangerous the better. She dislocated her shoulder ski-ing in Colorado, although it wasn't her fault. She was on a black run, which isn't quite the hardest sort (that's double-black), but was still a bit tougher than she would normally try. Unfortunately, a man of 6'4" came down the mountain, screaming at her to get out of the way, and "pummelled" into her.

She was in rather more danger during the holiday she took during the summer of 1996 to recuperate from the shoot. With Cruise and some friends, she decided to go on a yachting tour of the Italian coast, mooring near the active volcano, Stromboli. Cruise wasn't interested in joining her for a hike up to the top, so Nicole found herself a local guide who clearly wasn't too well-prepared. Instead of insisting that Nicole kit herself out properly – taking hiking boots, proper socks and some water would have been a good idea – he led Nicole up the mountain as she was, clad only in beige chinos and black sneakers.

By the time they reached the top, the sun was going down. At that point, Nicole now acknowledges, the trip crossed over from being merely

ABOVE: Julia Kelly and Thomas Devoe (George Clooney) run for their lives from an explosive situation in *The Peacemaker.*

dangerous to just plain stupid. The guide suggested they should take a different route down, descending the other side of the mountain – a quicker route, certainly during the day, but much more dangerous. It very quickly became impossible to see anything on the ash-covered mountain – and Nicole and the guide were stuck. One foot in the wrong place would lead to their deaths.

Some hours later, two Italian skydivers heard Nicole's cries for help and led the exhausted pair down the mountain to a couple's nearby yacht, where Nicole could finally call Cruise for help. "It was like one of those things out of a bad movie," she later recalled. "I was sobbing, 'Thomas,

her hosts had offered, Cruise knocked it back and hurried her home.

I just remember thinking, "So this is how I'm gonna go. Wow, I never would have predicted it to be this way." But now that I've survived it, I'm kind of proud of it. The people we were with said, "We're inviting you back! This is fun, this game: Celebrity Search and Rescue, we're gonna call it."

The Cruises were engaged in rescue work of a different kind – on Tom's reputation. The German magazine *Bunte* had produced a front-page story with a fabricated quote in which Cruise admitted that he was sterile. It was one thing for the stories to be bandied

RIGHT: Julia Kelly desperately makes her way through the new York streets to stop the nuclear explosion at the climax of *The Peacemaker*.

Thomas!'" Cruise ran the normally three-hour hike to the top of the mountain in an hour and a half, only to find that shock had made his wife very prim and proper. After she insisted that her husband accept the cup of coffee

around Hollywood verbally, but when Cruise was supposed to have said it himself, Tom and Nicole decided enough was enough and they would have to take action. Interviews they gave at the time still made it clear that the adoption of their children was an area about which they simply would not talk in any detail.

> I have two children that are the most exquisite creatures. Whether I give birth to a child or not, it's not even an element that exists now. If more are added to the family, more will be, but that's a very personal thing. It isn't anybody else's business.

Cruise filed a $60m lawsuit against *Bunte*, who immediately caved in and printed a front cover retraction. Cruise dropped the suit – but made it clear that he and Nicole would bring actions against anyone who went public with such slurs in the future.

Work on *The Portrait of a Lady* wasn't quite finished. Post-production of the film was carried out in Sydney, giving Nicole a chance to spend some time with her family. The ornate costumes Nicole had worn caused a problem when it came to the sound – the swishing of the dresses drowned out her performance, and a large proportion of the dialogue had to be re-recorded. This looping process sometimes required up to 20 takes to achieve a level of performance with which Nicole was satisfied. "She can be quite murderously challenging in her perfectionism," Campion said wryly once the process was complete.

It looked at this stage as if the Cruises' next film project would be a joint one. Some time earlier, famed film director Stanley Kubrick, whose reputation for directing great movies was almost as large as his reputation for perfectionism, had approached them simultaneously (by fax) and asked if they would be interested in working on a film called *Eyes Wide Shut*. A few months went by before

Kubrick was happy with the script, on which he was collaborating with novelist Frederic Raphael, at which stage he sent it to Cruise. According to Nicole, Tom "flipped" over the screenplay and, five days later, she read it herself and shared his opinion.

Eyes Wide Shut was to take up much of the next two years, with its delayed start, protracted shoot, and then the problems that arose when Kubrick died only days after delivering a print of the film to Warner Bros. But in the summer of 1996, it simply looked like an exciting project working with a fabulous director.

The intention had been to start filming *Eyes Wide Shut* that summer, once Nicole had recovered. However, for various reasons, Kubrick needed to push the start of filming back to the autumn, clearing Nicole's calendar unexpectedly. Nicole decided to fill the gap with something completely different.

The Peacemaker was the first film from a new studio in Hollywood – Dreamworks SKG, formed by the partnership of Steven Spielberg and Hollywood moguls Jeffrey Katzenberg and David Geffen. It was also an important movie for its lead, George Clooney, who was just beginning to lose the shackles of identification with his role on the top medical drama, *E.R. The Peacemaker* was a moderately straightforward thriller, culminating in the threat of a nuclear explosion in central New York City. Where it differed from run-of-the-mill, straight-to-video subjects was in its basis in the real-life Nuclear Smuggling Group, which was led by Dr Jessica Stern. Stern's character was fictionalised and became Julia Kelly, who has to work with Clooney's Colonel Devoe as they track down a missing nuclear weapon.

They weren't equal partners, even if the script tried to pretend they were, but they had a good working relationship.

Clooney wanted Nicole to play the part, and when he knew she was hesitant about accepting, called her and begged her to take it on. Nicole realised she had nothing to fear from an action film, and found it "fine but a little weird. So much of it is about the technical aspects rather than the performance." *The Peacemaker*'s director, Mimi Leder, recognised that Julia Kelly and Nicole Kidman shared an interest in being smart and precise, and knew that she would add immeasurably to the film.

Although Jane Campion has hinted in interviews that Nicole didn't enjoy her time on *The Peacemaker*, Nicole herself has always been exuberant about the fun she had during the filming. She wasn't going in expecting a major three-dimensional role that would fulfil her creatively: "I got to be the brains, George was the meat. I didn't want to be the girl pretending to be a guy running around with a gun."

The shoot took her out to Bratislava, a Slovakian city on the border of Austria and Hungary. Clooney finished work on the romantic comedy *One Fine Day*, opposite Michelle Pfeiffer, five days before shooting began on *The Peacemaker*, which meant there was no time for rehearsal. To his relief, he got on with Nicole in person immediately, and realised that she and Pfeiffer were both "about pure hard work ... Never a false word out of their mouths. You never think they're acting."

Nicole was glad that *The Peacemaker* offered her a chance to relax and have some fun. She wanted not to have to work every day, and be able to go out at night and dance, or go drinking with Clooney. Her co-star loved being able to go out, have fun bowling, knock back the local drink (borovicka), and then make joke phone calls to Tom Cruise, who was in the States filming *Jerry Maguire*. Nicole was a little worried that Clooney would make her the target of his beloved practical jokes, so decided to short-circuit the idea. She knew if she didn't do something, she'd constantly be worrying about when he would strike, so begged him for a truce. Clooney agreed – for as long as *The Peacemaker* was in production.

The Peacemaker opened in September 1997, by which time Cruise and Nicole were heavily involved in *Eyes Wide Shut*. When publicising the film, Nicole expressed herself very pleased with the change of pace it had offered her between Campion and Kubrick. Not that she was knocking Mimi Leder's work, or the character.

If she'd been a bumbling fool, which is how these characters are usually drawn, it might have been difficult. But I quite liked that she was right most of the time. Mimi wanted both the female and male characters to be wrong sometimes and right sometimes. And it was a working relationship, not about some romance, and I liked that about it too.

Dreamworks were satisfied with the film's performance: it made back its budget in overseas admissions alone, and the reviews were moderately favourable. For Nicole, it was a break before one of the most gruelling experiences of her life.

EYES WIDE SHUT

L OOKING back on 1996 for the Australian *Rolling Stone Yearbook*, Nicole said that it was a year she would always remember.

I got to see what I'd done in *Portrait of a Lady*, and then I got to work with Stanley Kubrick. I also continued to raise two children, and I was able to say "Happy sixth anniversary" to my husband.

There had been disappointments too. Nicole was very keen to appear in Gillian Armstrong's film of Peter Carey's novel *Oscar and Lucinda*. The screenplay was written by Laura Jones, who had served Nicole so well on *The Portrait of a Lady*, but Armstrong was keen to cast Cate Blanchett in the role of Lucinda Leplastrier.

I really wanted to do that, but they didn't want me. But you have to respect a director's decision about what they want. Casting comes from

ABOVE:
Alice and Bill Harford (Tom Cruise) prepare for an evening's entertainment in *Eyes Wide Shut*.

54

the gut and it's very important. I would have loved to have done that, but I'm thrilled that an Australian actress is doing it.

Tom and Nicole were clearly still in love; in his interviews publicising the release of *Mission: Impossible* Cruise regularly talked about his feelings for Nicole and the children, and it was this strength of feeling that Stanley Kubrick knew he could call upon during *Eyes Wide Shut*. As Cruise explained later, Kubrick might have told him and Nicole that it was simply an added bonus but, at heart, it was something he could count on and wanted.

Kubrick hadn't cast a 'movie star' in any of his films for some 20 years – not since Jack Nicholson terrorised Shelley Duvall in *The Shining*. But chairman Terry Semel at Warner Bros encouraged him to consider 'names' for the lead roles in *Eyes Wide Shut*. Kubrick had been working on the project on and off for many years – indeed, he first considered the source material, a 1926 novella called *Traumnovelle* by the Viennese writer Arthur Schnitzler, soon after completing work on *2001: A Space Odyssey* in 1968. Other projects caught his attention in the meantime, and he didn't return to it in earnest until the early 1990s.

Kubrick worked on the script with Frederic Raphael, who had written the screenplay for the 1967 adaptation of Thomas Hardy's *Far from the Madding Crowd* among many other highly regarded works. As Nicole and Tom were to discover, Kubrick operated in a similar way to Jane Campion: the script would be malleable, depending on the actors playing the roles. He would allow Nicole to ad-lib in front of the camera and then adapt the script accordingly.

Kubrick didn't start a film on a certain day, nor did he finish it on the day specified by the budget. He filmed when it was right to film, gave his cast regular days off (although no one was paid if they weren't shooting), and expected them to be available throughout the period of shooting, no matter how long that might be. On *Eyes Wide Shut*, this approach actually led to some scenes needing to be reshot, since Jennifer Jason Leigh was committed to the David Cronenberg film *eXistenZ* and couldn't return to Pinewood when she was needed unexpectedly by Kubrick. Nicole and Tom knew that they were committing themselves to an open-ended project – and they couldn't have been happier.

During filming of *Eyes Wide Shut*, the couple were bound by rules of absolute secrecy. Unsurprisingly, this meant that the rumour mill was rife; if you compiled all the rumours, you'd end up with a movie that was the absolute diametric opposite of what "Cruise, Kidman, Kubrick" (as the poster listed them) were up to. Nicole did squash one rumour – that she was playing a heroin addict – but otherwise, hard as it was for them, the Cruises kept quiet.

As was revealed when *Eyes Wide Shut* finally stunned audiences in July 1999, the Cruises play William and Alice Harford. He's a doctor, she's a failed art gallery owner. When they attend a grand pre-Christmas party, they are both tempted by attractive members of the opposite sex, but neither succumbs. They argue over why men are interested in Alice and, as the film progresses, we follow Bill through a sexual odyssey of different liaisons while Alice describes her sexual fantasies. Bill emerges from his experiences a lot wiser and, when he tells Alice everything that has happened, their argument is resolved and the marriage continues.

Both Tom and Nicole were nervous about meeting Kubrick for the first time, but by the time the dinner they were sharing at his home was over, Kubrick was busily telling Nicole all about his passion for Apple Macintosh computers. Nicole had been concerned that once the great director met her in person, he would realise that he had made a mistake. For she really wanted to work with him. She loved his work, although she admits she missed most of *The Shining* the first time round as she was making out with her boyfriend at the time. *Dr Strangelove*'s black comedy particularly appealed: "I suppose I just like laughing and at the same time feeling unnerved, and it's such a hard thing to do." Discovering that Kubrick had a "wonderful dry wit" helped Nicole relax, and even after the filming finished, the two remained constantly in touch until Kubrick's sudden death in 1999.

Kubrick didn't want Nicole to do her usual thorough research into the background of the movie she was about to make. He simply wanted her and her husband to get lost in the roles and their experiences together. The first day of rehearsals was nerve-wracking for Nicole but, just as she conquered and used her awe of John Malkovich in *The Portrait of a Lady*, she moved forward quickly.

> We were all sitting around, and I thought, "My God, Peter Sellers and Stanley used to sit together like this, discussing the script." That's when I got very intimidated. Once you start making a film, it becomes a different thing. Once you start working with someone, you can't keep them up on a pedestal. You just have to work,

otherwise it's detrimental because you don't take any risks and you don't feel free to say anything because you're worried about being seen as stupid. You have to discard that.

Nicole enjoyed working with Kubrick. The director much preferred to work with a small crew, making it more like collaborating on a student film than a massive Hollywood-backed project whose budget was threatening to spiral out of control. Kubrick had a reputation as a perfectionist, demanding dozens of takes from his actors. Nicole recognised that this was the mark of someone who was passionate about movies:

> You know you're working with someone who cares. He lives and breathes movies. And he makes so few that he enjoys the process that much more: he wants to exhaust all the possibilities. And the kind of actor that I am, I love that. I find it much harder to walk away with a director who says, "Hey, great, let's move on."

If anyone asked whether it was hell to work with Kubrick, Nicole would spring to his defence, claiming that it was an honour and that she would do it again in a second. She found Kubrick an extraordinary person. Since she wasn't in as many scenes in *Eyes Wide Shut* as Cruise, Nicole had more time on her hands during the shooting, and she would often go over to Kubrick's office just to be around him. Their discussions were wide-ranging – from politics to World War II, Peter Sellers to computers.

Kubrick welcomed the Cruises' input. When the set for Bill and Alice's bedroom was being decorated, Nicole

ABOVE:
Nicole laying bare
her body and her
emotions in *Eyes
Wide Shut.*

chose the books and the colour of the
window shades. She even added the
pocketful of loose change that Cruise
always left by the bedside table, and
put her own make-up and clothing
around the room. By the end of the shoot,
the room felt like home to both actors.

Because both Cruises were working
on the same movie, their usual rule
that the one not working looked after
the children was obviously impractical.
At times, Isabella and Connor would
simply spend some time in their
father's trailer, and then with their
mother, but when that proved impossible,
Cruise's mother came over to help out.

Because of the amount of free time
the very loose schedule gave her,
Nicole was able to spend time away
from the set and relax. She travelled to
London, Paris and Rome, and took the
opportunity to learn Italian. She also
spent a lot of time visiting the theatre,
during which time she met director
Sam Mendes, whose work at London's
Donmar Warehouse she really admired.
Their decision to work together was
the genesis of Nicole's triumphant
return to the stage in *The Blue Room*
in 1998.

Eyes Wide Shut's production seemed
to drag on interminably – at least as far
as the outside world was concerned.
Entertainment Weekly started running a
counter of how many days Cruise and
Kidman had been 'hostages' to the
movie. Nicole agreed subsequently that
there had been moments of frustration
when they wondered if it was ever
going to end, and Cruise pointed out
their concern that dealing for so long
with the themes of the film was like
handling dynamite. "We were both
dealing with jealousy and sex in a way
that it was always lurking around,"
Nicole added.

Some of the hardest moments to
film for Cruise and Kidman were the
intimate sexual ones. Not, as the *Star*
reported (and was promptly sued for
so doing), because the Cruises needed
any help in that department, but
simply because the scenes were so
sensitive. Nicole had always been
reticent about discussing such matters,
and it was only because of the
prevalence of rumours about Cruise's
sexuality that she had ever addressed
her bedroom activities in public. Now
she and Tom were about to go on
display in front of a camera. Both
Cruises had great admiration for the
sensitivity that Kubrick displayed.

It was just the three of us, sitting
in a room. He knew us and our
relationship as no one else does.
He'd say, "We're all on an equal level
here. We all throw ideas out. Some
will be laughable, some great. We've
all got to be willing to look like
idiots." So many times the
relationship with a director can
be an actor's nightmare. Ours was
incredible. It transcends making the
film. He changed my life so greatly,
inspired me, gave me confidence.

PRACTICAL MAGIC

IN late July 1997, before *Eyes Wide Shut* completed filming, Nicole nearly exited its cast in a rather unfortunate manner. *Vanity Fair* commissioned top photographer Annie Leibowitz to take a series of photos of Nicole at Virginia Woolf's sister's house, Charleston. Nicole had been able to arrange two days' clearance from the *Eyes Wide Shut* set to do the photos and accompanying interview. The main photos would be taken on the Thursday, then Nicole would fly home to the Cruises' current home in St Albans, have a good night's sleep, do the interview on the Friday morning, and then Leibowitz would take the cover photos on the Friday afternoon.

However, these plans were thrown out of kilter when the weather became really bad on Thursday evening while Nicole was being helicoptered home. The pilot narrowly avoided hitting a set of electricity lines and was forced to make an emergency landing in a remote part of the Home Counties. A bedraggled Nicole had to ask a startled farmer if she could use his phone, and didn't get home till 1.00 am. Although she could laugh at it the next day, Nicole was genuinely scared by the possibility of dying in such an accident.

The lesson was rammed home shortly afterwards, when Tom and

ABOVE: Gillian and Sally Owens (Sandra Bullock) dispose of an unwanted corpse in *Practical Magic*.

ABOVE:
Gillian Owens
enjoying the party
in *Practical Magic*.

Nicole were among the mourners at the funeral of Princess Diana, killed in a car crash in Paris a mere month later. The actors had got to know the

Princess after she attended the Royal premiere of *Far and Away* five years earlier, and had found a kindred spirit in her dislike of the attentions of the paparazzi.

When they did finally finish work on Kubrick's movie, it would be another 15 months before either Cruise would be allowed to see any footage. In the same way that she balanced the rigours of *The Portrait of a Lady* with the less strenuous emotional demands of *The Peacemaker*, Nicole now moved on to a very different film, the witchcraft comedy-thriller *Practical Magic*.

In common with many other actors, Nicole doesn't normally like watching her own movies – when *The Portrait of a Lady* turned up on cable television while the Cruises were filming *Eyes Wide Shut*, she begged Tom to change the channel. When she came to publicise *Practical Magic*, Nicole was pleasantly surprised to find that interviewers enjoyed the film, since she had had a great deal of fun making it.

> Usually when you've had a good experience, the movie doesn't look like it was a good experience at all. It's some strange law. But in this regard we had a great time.

She joined the other women in the cast – Sandra Bullock, Dianne Wiest and Stockard Channing – in the San Juan islands off the coast of Washington State, which were standing in for the film's New England location. Nicole plays Gillian Owens, with Bullock as her sister Sally, who were both brought up as witches by their aunts (Channing and Wiest). The female line is cursed – anyone who loves an Owens woman will die. When Sally's husband succumbs to the curse, Gillian, who's been pursuing a carefree existence, comes home to comfort her. Unfortunately, her latest boyfriend is abusing her and, when Sally goes to her rescue, they end up killing him – but he refuses to stay dead, eventually possessing Gillian...

Sandra Bullock had enjoyed the Alice Hoffman novel on which the film is based and thought that it would be a perfect project for her to work on with Nicole, even though the two had never worked together before and didn't really know each other. Bullock brought director Griffin Dunne on board and they prepared the script. However, Nicole was still tied up with *Eyes Wide Shut* and there was pressure on Bullock to consider other people for the role of Gillian. Bullock was not prepared to compromise the film – she had learned from the disastrous performance of *Speed 2: Cruise Control* that it was a mistake to start a film until all the elements were in place. Hence, the production was delayed. When asked why she was so firm about casting Nicole, Bullock would simply reply, "Just because..."

The two women spent a lot of time together during the shooting of *Practical Magic* and Bullock was quite surprised to find that, in the end, they had nothing in common, although they got on extremely well. They enjoyed each other's company because they were so unlike. In the middle of the usual difficulties that any film has – particularly one shooting in the spring in the cold of the northern United States – both found it comforting to have someone to turn to and discuss totally normal things with. Nicole and Bullock were regularly found sitting down at a table with a bottle of wine, chatting about boys, kids and clothes.

The roles were equal, and the film was unusual in having two female leads. Griffin Dunne found that the collaboration of the two women made it easier to pull off a film whose tone he described as a "feminist mix of *Rosemary's Baby* and *Bewitched*."

The women all enjoyed themselves while they were making the film, although in the scene where the aunts and nieces get drunk together, they were all drinking water on camera. After filming was finished for the day, they decided to enact it for real. "I should say that we were the wildest things to ever hit the island, but I don't think we were," Nicole commented later.

Sandra Bullock had a chance to see the proof of how happy the Cruises were when Tom paid his wife a surprise visit. He flew over with flowers and videos, and the pair spent the weekend together.

When he left, he flew really low over the set and tipped his wing, like he was saying goodbye to her! Every woman on the set was ready to gouge out their eyes. Now, if that's a marriage of convenience, then I would like to be conveniently married to a guy like that!

The lack of information about *Eyes Wide Shut* before the film's release meant that interviews with both Tom and Nicole now concentrated more than ever on their domestic life. Nicole commented that she understood Paul McCartney's grief following his wife Linda's death from cancer, because she really understood the relationship that the McCartneys had shared. "I don't know what I would do without Tom," she commented, while Cruise added that the line "You complete me," which he had to say at the end of *Jerry Maguire*, summed up exactly how he felt about Nicole.

The two revealed how much they had learned from each other. Although Nicole was trying to calm down some of her excesses now that she was a mother as well as a wife, she still enjoyed participating in dangerous sports.

> Before Tom, I was never a skier, and now I love it. He taught me how to ride a trail bike and next we are going to learn rock climbing. We love to drive go-karts: it's addictive! Sometimes we do it until two in the morning. We also go scuba diving and skydiving, which is the most incredible adrenaline buzz.

But the couple were still getting the greatest buzz from being parents. If they worked late and the children were in bed when they got home, they would get them up, bring them into their bed, watch TV, snuggle and eat ice cream!

They didn't neglect their friends either. If someone couldn't afford to travel to join them wherever in the world they were, the Cruises would fork out for the plane fare, or go and collect them themselves. Nicole loved throwing parties – basketball-themed ones for Cruise (particularly if they were out of the country and he was getting withdrawal symptoms from his favourite games), New Year's Eve boat parties for her Australian friends and family, and incredible theme parties for everyone else. She cemented her friendship with Sandra Bullock by throwing her a Moroccan-themed party, complete with camels, belly dancers and snake charmers. "Nicole is

a direct split between royalty and a 15-year-old girl," Bullock commented. "But the 15-year-old girl rarely gets seen in public."

The Cruises and their lawyers maintained a careful eye on the tabloids, as the *Sunday Express* discovered when they ran a story claiming that the Cruises' marriage was a sham to hide the fact that Tom was gay. The paper had to pay an undisclosed sum – which the Cruises forwarded to charity – and make a public apology, saying that the story was entirely false.

Anyone listening to Nicole wouldn't need further convincing. She wasn't pretending that everything was wonderful all the time – but she wouldn't change it for anything.

> I have happiness with this person. Or I have both happiness and unhappiness with him. It's a complicated relationship but I'm glad it's complicated, because otherwise I'd be bored. It's been nine years and I'm past the seven year itch. When you're loved for your flaws, that's when you really feel safe. I have a lot of flaws, and I'm difficult to live with, and he still loves me.

ABOVE: A tense moment between lovers in one of the sequences in *The Blue Room.*

LEFT: Ian Glen enjoys the view in *The Blue Room.*

THE BLUE ROOM

tempted by the idea of producing a contemporary version of *La Ronde*, a Schnitzler play which was itself derived from *Traumnouvelle*, the source of *Eyes Wide Shut*. Mendes knew that if he was going to work on a project with Nicole, it would need to be something that challenged them both.

If there were still any doubts about Nicole's dedication to the art of acting, *The Blue Room* should have put paid to them. She and Cruise had already turned down a lot of well-paid roles because of their commitment to the over-running *Eyes Wide Shut*, and now she took on a role on the London stage for Equity minimum – £250 per week.

She was back on familiar territory – working in a rehearsal room, discovering a new character, or in this case five new characters. *The Blue Room* charts a series of sexual intrigues between five men and five women. Nicole played all the women, from a 17-year-old prostitute to an imperious actress in her mid-forties, while her co-star Iain Glen played, among others, a taxi driver, a callow student and a philandering politician. Glen was a member of the Royal Shakespeare Company who would follow his triumph alongside Nicole in London and on Broadway with the part of Manfred Powell in *Lara Croft, Tomb Raider*! Each of the five pairings flung their clothes off and coupled during onstage blackouts, to the accompaniment of an electric buzzer and a sign that told the audience the length of their liaison.

Nicole loved this opportunity to experiment, do something new and take risks. She saw the play as being about "identity, desire, fidelity and the way in which people present

To play with emotional dynamite once is risky; to choose to play with it a second time might be seen as suicidal. But that's what Nicole decided to do when she returned to the stage in *The Blue Room*.

David Hare's play wasn't just dealing with the same themes as *Eyes Wide Shut* – it was even derived from material by the same author, Arthur Schnitzler. Hare, one of the most respected British playwrights, was approached by Sam Mendes after the Donmar Warehouse-based director had forged a friendship with Nicole during the filming of *Eyes Wide Shut*. Hare was

themselves to each other." All of
the characters' nuances had to be
presented by the actors themselves,
without aid of ageing make-up
(there simply wasn't time to go off
stage to have it applied), so Nicole's
experiences of playing different ages
stood her in good stead.

The rehearsal process also led Nicole
into a new realm of shared intimacy.
She and Glen worked out between
them exactly what level of intimacy
each of the couples they were
portraying had reached. During
rehearsals, they didn't even kiss.
They simply touched hands and shared
details from their own experiences to
fill in the gaps. Nicole found herself
telling Glen things she hadn't shared
with anyone else in her life.

Hare used the original play *La Ronde*
as the basis for a "more modern, maybe
more romantic view of sexual
yearning" and spent some time during
the rehearsal period ensuring that the
parts were really effective for the actors
playing them.

> It was a process I really enjoyed, a
> bit of bespoke tailoring fitted for
> Nicole and Iain Glen. I was choosing
> a few cuts, fitting the collar to the
> actor. That's good fun as a
> playwright – seeing what you see in
> the actor and bringing it out. With
> Nicole, I saw a great sweetness in
> her, which is generally missed. You
> often see her as an ice maiden or
> lofty or unattainable, and one thing
> I tried to do was make it warmer as
> it went on.

Nicole rarely thinks that anything she
has done is going to succeed, and *The
Blue Room* was no exception. Not long
before the play opened in London, she
phoned her father in Sydney, panicking

that she wouldn't be able to do all
the different accents and portray the
characters accurately. Antony Kidman
knew how to handle his daughter and
spent 45 minutes helping her to come
to the conclusion that she would be
able to deal with it after all.

One feature of the play that Nicole
didn't seem to have much of a problem
with was her brief onstage nudity. She
had made enough nude appearances

ABOVE:
Dressing the part
for *The Blue Room*.

on screen over the years to be comfortable with her body in the fleeting scene where Glen's self-adoring playwright dresses her after they have made love. Unsurprisingly, it was this scene that attracted most attention from the press and public, with the *Daily Telegraph*'s Charles Spencer describing her as "pure theatrical Viagra".

Hare himself was amazed by Nicole's performance. At the dress rehearsal, he could still take note of Nicole's technical limitations, but by the time the play opened two weeks later, they were gone.

ABOVE:
At the Westwood Village Premiere of *Eyes Wide Shut* on 13 July 1999.

In two weeks she'd been to university and learned how to be a stage actress. You don't see that richness of physical texture in British acting, that incredible amount of brush strokes. There was a famous saying about John Gielgud that he acted from the neck up. Nicole acts all the way down.

The play was a sell-out for its run from 22 September to 31 October, with ticket touts able to command £1000 for not particularly good seats. Spencer's

review passed into legend, but others joined him in praising Nicole's "achingly beautiful" looks coupled with her "bravura, skill and real feeling". It was clear: she wasn't simply a star name brought to the London stage – she was really delivering the goods.

While she was preparing for her London debut, Nicole was also working on another new phase in her career, as a producer. She had read Suzanne Moore's very graphic novel *In The Cut*, and found it very appealing. "It speaks to a generation of women in their thirties now who are lonely," she explained. Nicole decided to buy the rights and present them to Jane Campion as a project for them to work on together. She had faith in Campion's ability to bring the themes of the book to the screen without going into all the graphic detail that Moore uses in the book; "I've never known Jane to be ugly in the way she depicts sex", she said. As they worked on the book, Nicole and Campion discovered that they were becoming increasingly passionate about it and determined that, though it was a very controversial novel, the film version would not be made to shock.

It came as little surprise when *The Blue Room* transferred to Broadway, opening at the Cort Theater on 13 December 1998. New Yorkers flocked to the play just as British audiences had, and Nicole gave her all for the performances. In fact, she gave a little too much; she had to bow out of the final week's performances when she contracted laryngitis. She felt devastated, particularly as her voice actually disappeared while she was on stage, screaming in character. She already had a cold, and suddenly nothing came out.

It was a surreal moment – gone! The voice was just gone. There was just nothing. And as an actor, it's the most horrifying thing, because I then get into the whole panic. I'm like out of Woody Allen where, oh no, that means it'll never come back. It means there's something dreadfully wrong with her voice.

Luckily, that didn't prove to be the case, and Nicole was sensible enough to stop before she did permanent damage.

One of Nicole's backstage visitors during the Broadway run of *The Blue Room* was destined to play an important role in her future – Australian director Baz Luhrmann. At that stage he was putting together his ideas for *Moulin Rouge!* and recognised Nicole's talents. If she could sing for prolonged periods as well as she could act, then they could definitely work together.

Many others recognised the special qualities that Nicole brought to *The Blue Room*. Her London performance was rewarded with the *Evening Standard*'s Special Award and she was nominated for a prestigious Laurence Olivier Award for the Broadway run.

In the week when she should have been finishing her run on Broadway in triumph, Nicole and Tom Cruise finally got to see their performances in *Eyes Wide Shut*. A cinema was hired in Manhattan at the start of March 1999 and the projectionist was ordered to turn his back so he didn't see the film that was unspooling on the screen – only Cruise and Kidman were allowed to watch. When it came to an end, Cruise insisted that they should watch it again. Only then did they leave. Nicole's voice wasn't strong enough to call Kubrick to tell him what she thought and, to her despair, when it returned and she rang his home in

England, she was told that Kubrick had died of a heart attack during the night. Her period without a voice was the longest time since the completion of *Eyes Wide Shut* that Nicole hadn't spoken with Kubrick, whom she described as being like a father to her.

For everyone else, Stanley was mysterious. For me he was solid, kind, so caring. He understood your humanity and revelled in your dedication.

The Cruises immediately took on the mantle of protectors of *Eyes Wide Shut*, declaring that if anyone wanted to make changes to Kubrick's work posthumously, they would have to deal with them as well. As it happened, Terry Semel and Robert Daly, the co-chairmen of Warner Bros, had seen the film a mere three days before Kubrick's death and had told him they were blown away by it. Semel admitted he breathed a sigh of relief when he realised that the film was sexy rather than pornographic, since an NC-17 rating in America would have been the kiss of death. Even so, when the film was finally aired, there were some brief masking effects used in American prints to disguise some of the sexual activity during the orgy sequence.

Although reviews of *Eyes Wide Shut* varied from describing it as "an astonishing work made with masterful control" to "a dismal and overwrought piece of work", Nicole was more interested in the reactions of others in the industry. Sam Mendes spent an hour and a half chatting with her and Tom after he'd seen it; Martin Scorsese was babbling about Kubrick's genius on display, while Steven Spielberg simply told her that "It's the best thing you've ever done."

All the praise encouraged Nicole to forge ahead with her next major role, as the ill-fated Satine in *Moulin Rouge!*.

OPPOSITE:
Nicole poses, complete with high heels, at the *Eyes Wide Shut* premiere in July 1999.

BIRTHDAY GIRL

LIKE *In the Cut*, one of Nicole's other projects in 1999 was destined not to see the light of day until 2002. *Birthday Girl* was unusual in another respect: although it is set in St Albans in the heart of Hertfordshire, it was partly filmed in Sydney Australia.

The film began shooting in June 1999, with Nicole starring as mail-order Russian bride Nadia, who brings love, chaos and mayhem to the life of her intended – mild-mannered bank clerk John Buckingham, played by Ben Chaplin. When she arrives, he realises that the 'From Russia With Love' website wasn't absolutely accurate about her grasp of English. In fact, she only knows the word 'yes'. After some false starts, they begin to communicate through the international language of highly charged sex, before her cousins arrive for her birthday. At this point the film becomes more serious, as Nadia is taken hostage by one of her cousins, who insists that John rob his own bank.

Nicole read the script and decided that she really wanted to play the part of Nadia. Just as Gus Van Sant couldn't initially imagine Nicole in the role of Suzanne Stone Moretto for *To Die For*, now writer-director Jez Butterworth couldn't quite see the international movie star working on his small-scale movie. Particularly as her husband Tom Cruise was working on *Mission: Impossible 2*, which was shooting in Australia, and they had their well-known rule about not being separated for more than two weeks at any one time.

Nicole knew that she was asking Butterworth to take a risk in casting her as a Russian, but she promised him that she would do the "appropriate work", which included being able to speak Russian. It wouldn't be good enough simply to

LEFT:
A smile for the cameras as *Birthday Girl* is finally premiered on 21 November 2001 at the Odeon, Leicester Square, London.

be able to say the scripted words in a convincing Russian accent – Nicole wanted to be able to improvise in Russian, if that's what her director wanted.

Both problems were solved. The decision was made to shoot the first part of the film in Sydney, so the Cruises could work on their respective movies. Filming in Sydney had the added advantage that co-star Ben Chaplin could also spend time with his sister, who was based in the Australian city.

Miramax, who were producing *Birthday Girl*, assisted with Nicole's vocal requirements; Liz Himelstein, a highly regarded voice coach, was made available throughout the shoot, and Nicole enjoyed showing off her new language to interviewers. Producer Diana Phillips was delighted with the results, claiming at the start of filming that Nicole's performance was "beyond expectations. I think she's the real thing. When the film comes out, people will be mightily impressed."

Butterworth admitted that he was dubious about casting Nicole because he thought there was every chance her celebrity might overbalance the rest of the film. However, once they met, it became obvious to him that Nicole's celebrity was irrelevant – she was a keen actor who wanted to be challenged by a role, and the part of Nadia fitted the bill. "Her wish to take risks was irresistible," he added.

No doubt influenced by the stories that were still circulating regarding Nicole's demands on set, Butterworth had a quiet chat with his star before filming began.

> I said, "Look, I've directed lots of actors before, but I've never directed a movie star. Is it any different?" She said no, and that was that really.

Ben Chaplin also enjoyed working with Nicole on the movie, particularly the sex scenes.

> Nicole is great. She's very used to love scenes. In *Birthday Girl*, probably one twentieth of the racy stuff we shot made it into the movie. I found I lost my cherry on that one. I came out a veteran of sex scenes. Nicole was absolutely professional, but there was no coyness. She's very free. And if you're free and understand that it's part of the job then you can actually get creative with the sex scenes.

Although shooting wrapped on *Birthday Girl* after five weeks of exteriors in St Albans, further scenes were necessary, and Nicole slotted them in after she finished work on *Moulin Rouge!*.

Miramax decided to hold the film back from general release until 2002, although it was premiered at the London Film Festival in November 2001. It received generally good reviews, with the *LA Times* commenting that Nicole was "convincingly Slavic and always entertaining ... [she] has considerable fun as the strong-minded intrepid woman no man can resist."

Nicole's work on *Birthday Girl*, and subsequently *Moulin Rouge!*, meant that the nomadic wanderings of the Cruises came to a temporary halt, and they started to put down a few roots. There was another, personal reason for the Cruises' move to Australia – they were safer there from the prying eyes of the paparazzi. After Princess Diana's death, Nicole came out to Australia and was hounded by the press. In an effort to get some peace for her family, especially the children, she went on a radio show and actually asked if the press could leave her family alone so the children could have a normal life. Rather to everyone's surprise, they responded to her plea, and the Cruises accordingly felt that "Australia is the easiest country for us to be in."

Nicole and Tom were still keen that the children should be left to be themselves, and Nicole found herself quoting Hilary Rodham Clinton, who said that she wanted to let her daughter Chelsea define herself before she was defined by other people.

> We want Bella and Connor both to have the chance to define themselves before we have defined them in the press or through anybody. They will probably battle us – we don't take them to premieres, we don't take them to anything – but they still have a very full, fun life. They just don't have a public life.

The Cruises enjoyed the Australian lifestyle, and it also gave them an opportunity to experience new things in their pursuit of the extreme, such as swimming with Great White sharks (in a cage, naturally) off the coast of South Australia.

There must have been times during her next project when Nicole felt that swimming with sharks was probably a much safer bet than what her director was asking of her. For, as she memorably described Baz Luhrmann's direction, "It's almost like Baz takes you to the side of the cliff and just pushes you off. You just say, 'I hope that there's water down there.'

MOULIN ROUGE!

MOULIN ROUGE!

BAZMARK ANTHONY LUHRMANN came into Nicole's life five years before *Moulin Rouge!* went in front of the cameras at Fox's Sydney studios in November 1999. He and his wife Catherine Martin, who acted as production and costume designer on *Moulin Rouge!*, were asked to 'guest edit' an issue of Australian *Vogue*. They decided to do a series of fashion sittings, including a musical-comedy series, and enlisted Nicole. To their surprise, they discovered that Nicole could portray a lightness of touch and still be glamorous. Martin realised that Luhrmann had brought out "that aspect of being a comedienne in the fabulous sense of the word, that ability to be funny and glamorous simultaneously, which I think is quite difficult."

Luhrmann had built a reputation as a director who would take risks and succeed simply by virtue of pushing his ideas to the limit. *William Shakespeare's Romeo + Juliet* entranced audiences who otherwise would have walked away from the Bard. With *Moulin Rouge!*, he completed a trilogy of films begun with *Strictly Ballroom* where excess ruled and a manic energy seemed to govern the characters.

We are setting out to evolve further the cinematic style we began developing with *Strictly Ballroom* and *Romeo + Juliet*. This style is defined by setting a mythical story structure in a heightened world and by telling the story through an expressive device such as dance, or in the case of *Romeo + Juliet* a 400-year-old language. The device I am exploring with this project is music and song.

OPPOSITE: Satine ponders an uncertain fuutre at the *Moulin Rouge!*

BELOW: The enticing line-up at the *Moulin Rouge!* lead by Harold Zidler (Jim Broadbent).

After Luhrmann watched Nicole's performance in *The Blue Room* on Broadway, he sent her a box of long-stemmed red roses together with a note that read, "She sings! She dances! She dies..." Those were the requirements for Satine, and Luhrmann hoped that he had found someone who could fulfil them. The two latter requirements were definitely not a problem for an actress of Nicole's wide range, and he had heard a little bit of her singing voice briefly during *The Blue Room.*

Nicole was asked to audition, and she prepared the theme tune from the James Bond movie, *The Spy Who Loved Me – Nobody Does It Better.* Marvin Hamlisch's song won over Luhrmann, who cast her as Satine. He had always wanted to work with her "because she has so much more to reveal" – and

distinctly late-20th century ambience to it. As Satine, Nicole entices Ewan McGregor's innocent poet, Christian, and he tries to save her from the seedy world of the nightclub and its Can Can show, Spectacular Spectacular. But one fatal jealous mistake means that Christian loses Satine forever.

Making *Moulin Rouge!* wasn't ever going to be easy. From the start, Nicole was aware that it was going to be a very demanding shoot. Luhrmann insisted that Nicole and McGregor devote months of their lives to workshopping and preparing for their roles. For two and a half weeks, Nicole and McGregor worked with Luhrmann, going through the various songs and seeing how the chemistry between them worked. At the end of that time, the director invited what he

LEFT:
Part of the spectacle surrounding Satine and Christian (Ewan McGregor) *in Moulin Rouge!*

there were few of Nicole's talents that weren't revealed during *Moulin Rouge!'s* production.

The film was a retelling of the Greek myth of Orpheus in the Underworld, transposed to the late-19th century Moulin Rouge club in Paris, but with a

described as "a few people" round to see how his potential stars were doing. Nicole felt very exposed but accepted it as part of the challenge of the part.

The reaction was favourable, and the film moved further into production. Nicole and McGregor worked with

Luhrmann's voice coach, Andrew Ross. Nicole was still not confident that she would be able to carry off the amount of singing required of her in the part, particularly as Luhrmann was insisting that she would be singing live in the studio, rather than miming to pre-recorded backing tracks. Ross encouraged her to have faith in herself – after all, as he pointed out to her, Luhrmann would not have cast her if he didn't think that she was capable of the role. He had been auditioning worldwide to find Satine, and he had chosen Nicole.

The intention was never to turn Nicole into an opera singer, even if there were times when she was singing what were essentially operatic cues. However, everyone working on the project was aware that Luhrmann would demand ever more from them, and there were moments when both leads felt exposed.

Nicole wanted to do her homework, and on this occasion that meant watching many of the great screen musicals. Her film diet included the work of Rita Hayworth, Marilyn Monroe, Cyd Charisse, Ginger Rogers and Marlene Dietrich, and she came away from the experience with the utmost respect for their talents.

I used to love Katharine Hepburn, but now, although I still do, my hat goes off to those other women who could sing and dance and act – they were phenomenal. It also opened up a whole new door for me because, before, my parents liked musicals and I thought, "Oh yeah, right," but now I've watched a lot, I appreciate the talent it takes to make a great musical.

Each day during the rehearsal period McGregor and Nicole would take dance lessons, learning or upgrading their knowledge of the salsa and the mambo, then go to singing lessons before spending a couple of hours on improvisation classes with Luhrmann. Nicole felt that she had gone back to drama school, but understood what Luhrmann was trying to achieve.

Baz is the kind of director who pushes you early on in the piece, so that by the time you start to film, you're so comfortable with what you're doing, you're ready to do anything.

Filming began in early November 1999 and almost immediately ground to a halt when Nicole fractured two ribs. It was almost impossible to shoot in her absence, so production went on hiatus until 25 November. Tragedy then struck on the very morning they started back up: as Luhrmann went to give the cue for action, one of the crew brought over a cellphone with the news that Luhrmann's father had died.

The pressure of the corset that Nicole had to wear was partly the cause of her cracked ribs; her body simply couldn't cope with being lifted aloft while so tightly laced. For a time, Nicole and Catherine Martin considered changing the costume so that Nicole wouldn't need the corset, but it would possibly have compromised the film. Although she didn't wear it while her ribs healed, Nicole was soon laced back up, and took regular advantage of a leaning board so that she didn't have to try to sit down.

Putting those early setbacks behind them, the cast and crew eventually filled Fox's Sydney studios with the most outlandish designs and ideas.

One of Luhrmann's favourite rallying cries was to dare the performers to make him tell them that they were overdoing it. He never had to throughout the shoot.

Satine has a number of set pieces in the movie, one of which is a redefinition of Marilyn Monroe's famous song, *Diamonds are a Girl's Best Friend*. Nicole found the sequence a nightmare to shoot, because she simply wasn't sure how it would work in the context of the film, and she was setting herself up for comparison with Monroe's iconic performance.

There's something to be said about throwing yourself into it and going, "OK Baz, you think it's going to work... Great!"

Luhrmann and Nicole worked on various different interpretations and in the end went with a version that is raunchier than Monroe's, using more of a chest voice and a less breathy delivery. Nicole loved Luhrmann's feeling that anything was possible in the movie – although she was also fond of describing him as "breathtakingly naïve".

Nicole was determined that she would do as many of her own stunts as she possibly could, especially her entrance from the ceiling on a trapeze. It was a moment that will live with her forever – combining cinematic spectacle with her love of danger. It was being shot at 11.00 pm and, knowing how much her parents loved musicals, Nicole got her father out of bed to come to the set so he could experience the moment for himself.

I got up onto this trapeze, with all these men in tuxedos below, and Baz calling out things like "All right,

men, we want unbridled lust", and they'd be screaming and cheering and throwing their hats. I'd be looking down at them from up on the trapeze, and I'd go "Remember this moment."

Late in the shoot, Nicole suffered another accident, requiring her to have knee surgery. Unfortunately there was no longer the possibility of the production closing down to allow her a chance to recuperate. The new *Star Wars* movie was booked into the studio from the middle of April and Ewan McGregor had to finish his work on *Moulin Rouge!* before unsheathing his lightsabre once more. Nicole knew that she had to keep going, come what may.

Nicole shone throughout the making of *Moulin Rouge!* and her pleasure in the role shows on screen. She loved the opportunity to play a tragic heroine.

Of course, I'd love to do a love story in which I get to live, but the classic arc of the woman who finally gets to meet the person she's waited for her whole life, but she's dying at the same time – it's the classic combination and a great arc for an actress to play.

By the time that *Moulin Rouge!* had completed post-production and was ready for unveiling at the Cannes Film Festival, the film itself wasn't the centre of attention – for Nicole Kidman's life was about to undergo its most radical upheaval to date.

OPPOSITE:
Partnered by Ewan McGregor at the *Moulin Rouge!* premiere at the Cannes Film Festival on 9 May 2001.

DEVASTATION

DEVASTATION

ABOVE:
One of Tom and
Nicole's last public
appearances
together at the
Venice Film
Festival in 1999.

All I can say is that I hope we are together when we are 80. I can't say we will be, but I will be so devastated if we're not.

SPEAKING more openly than usual to Australian magazine *Talk* in its September 2000 issue, Nicole for the first time was expressing some doubts about her and Cruise's relationship. Elsewhere in the interview she discussed the fact she was 'high maintenance' and that when she had PMS she was very difficult to live with. Previously she had checked herself from saying for certain that she and Cruise would be together for the rest of their lives, not wanting to tempt fate, but now there were a few hints that not everything was as solid at home as it had been before.

When a marriage breaks up, only two people really know what went on, and the Cruises' separation and divorce, even though it was conducted in a very public arena, was no different. Tensions were clearly evident between the couple on the set of *The Others*, which Cruise was producing and Nicole was starring in. The buzz on *Moulin Rouge!* was that it was going to be a major success – Fox decided to hold it back from release so that Baz Luhrmann had ample time to realise his vision for the movie – and it was very evident that Nicole's career was on the verge of a new phase.

At one stage, rumour had it that she was even going to be entering the field of athletics, carrying the Olympic torch to open the 2000 Olympics being held in Sydney that September. Nicole didn't want to give credence to the rumour, but unfortunately her lack

of a denial meant that even more people believed it was true. It was only when TV commentators started lambasting her for taking the honour away from a genuine athlete that Nicole forcefully denied she had ever been approached. She was fired up by patriotism during the Olympics and admitted that she became starstruck when she met Australia's top swimmer, Ian Thorpe.

Her next role, in *The Others*, took Nicole into chiller territory. She played Grace, the overprotective mother of two children who suffer from xeroderma pigmentosum, a rare disease that means they're allergic to light. However, as increasingly strange

ABOVE:
Grace Stewart
wonders if she
and her and her
children are under
threat from
The Others.

things happen, Grace begins to wonder if she and her children are really alone in the house.

For *The Others*, Nicole and family left Sydney to travel to Madrid, even though the film was set in the Channel Islands. The director, Alejandro

OPPOSITE: Nicole gives her side of the story after the split from Tom Cruise is announced.

Amenábar, was Spanish, and *The Others* was his first English-speaking film. Amenábar had built a solid reputation with his Spanish films; his 1997 hit *Abre los ojos* (*Open Your Eyes*) was ironically the basis for *Vanilla Sky*, Tom Cruise's first film after his separation from Nicole.

Although she described *The Others* as a "funky film" in public, Nicole later admitted that she had been hesitant about accepting the role.

> At one point I was even trying to come up with a list of actresses to replace me. That's how desperate I was not to do it. I'd just come off doing *Moulin Rouge!* where I got to sing and fall in love, and suddenly I was going to step into this very dark world. But [Amenábar] really encouraged me to do it.

Another problem materialised when Nicole arrived in Spain – her knee injury sustained during the shooting of *Moulin Rouge!* was causing her considerable problems, and she had to fly to Los Angeles to have it scanned. Luckily, she was deemed fit to continue, and returned to the location at El Palacio de los Hornillos in the Cantabria region of Northern Spain.

Nicole was glad that she persevered. Grace wasn't a simple character by any definition. Amenábar called her "a castrating mother – she loves her children madly." Nicole was keen that by the end of the movie the audience should have some sympathy with her, and certainly seemed to have succeeded as far as influential critic Roger Ebert was concerned: "Nicole Kidman succeeds in convincing us that she is a normal person in a disturbing situation and not just a standard-issue horror movie hysteric."

Christmas Eve 2000 marked Tom and Nicole's tenth wedding anniversary. It later became a bone of contention between them as to whether they were still together on that day or whether the separation had already happened; under Californian law, Nicole's claim on Cruise became much larger if they had achieved ten years of marriage. According to the court papers that Nicole filed in response to Cruise's petition for divorce in February 2001:

> The parties had happily celebrated their tenth wedding anniversary with a group of friends. During the balance of December and thereafter, the parties were intimate.

According to Nicole, Cruise was still living with her during January, when she was forced to pull out of David Fincher's new film, *Panic Room*. Her knee injury flared up again and she had to be replaced by Jodie Foster. The role called on the heroine to be quite athletic, and Nicole knew that she could cause further and perhaps irreparable damage if she pushed her knee too far. As a favour to Fincher, however, she did make a brief uncredited appearance in the movie, as a voice on the phone.

Cruise dropped his bombshell on 4 February 2001. Nicole urged him not to leave; they could try marriage counselling or "take other steps to

ABOVE:
Attending an international premiere of *The Others* at Halloween 2001

address whatever problems may have existed in their marriage." Cruise reportedly refused to listen, said his decision was final, and left home.

The next day, publicists for both Nicole and Cruise announced that the couple were splitting up after ten years of marriage. As ever in such circumstances, everyone involved claimed that it was "an amicable separation" and that there were no current plans to take it any further.

That might have been Nicole's belief, but it certainly wasn't Cruise's. On 7 February, he filed for divorce on the grounds of irreconcilable differences which, the divorce papers stated, were connected to their careers. The press went wild, speculating that Cruise's belief in Scientology had forced them apart; although Nicole was herself a member of the Church of Scientology, she had made it clear in interviews that it wasn't the foremost force in her life. The *New York Post* reported that Cruise and the Scientologists had tried to save the marriage, but Nicole wanted to raise the children as Catholics.

Nicole was totally shocked by Cruise's actions – he was dealing with her as ruthlessly as he had dealt with Mimi Rogers 11 years earlier. As far as she was concerned, they had only just renewed their marriage vows and, although she knew there were problems with their marriage, she had no idea that Cruise felt it was over. Her family flew over to console her, support she particularly needed when she lost the baby that she was carrying. She maintained that the child was Cruise's but that he didn't make any contact with her.

As she recovered from the loss of her child, Nicole maintained a low profile, although she did authorise her publicist to confirm that she had miscarried. Her first priority remained looking after Isabella and Connor, but as the Cannes Film Festival approached she realised that she would have to face the world's press for the premiere of *Moulin Rouge!*.

Speaking just before she left Los Angeles for Cannes, she admitted that she was nervous about facing the press.

I've always been a very cards-on-the-table person and I'm used to being able to talk about all parts of my life very openly and freely, but I suppose it is about 'The Show Must Go On' and it's about being professional and supporting Baz and the film ... It's strange because it's the best and worst time in my life coming together.

She needn't have worried. Although there were the inevitable questions about Cruise, his new relationship with *Vanilla Sky* co-star Penelope Cruz, and her miscarriage, Nicole carried them off with a bravura performance, relying on the support of Baz Luhrmann. The film itself amazed audiences when they saw it and Nicole's enthusiasm for it remained unabated. She even saw a message in it for herself: 'It is better to have loved and lost than never to have loved at all.'

Nicole continued working. *In The Cut* was in pre-production, although she and Campion received a blow when Miramax put the project into turnaround, which effectively meant cancelling it. The production company claimed that they were looking for a "dark thriller in the vein of *Se7en*", while Campion saw the film in more of a "darkly romantic" vein. However, Pathe International picked up the rights and the film's future seemed more certain.

On the other side of the camera, Nicole was preparing for her role in *The Hours*, in which she was playing the writer Virginia Woolf. David Hare, the author of *The Blue Room*, had scripted the film for director Stephen Daldry. The picture had been intended for shooting earlier in 2001 but it was put back to June, with a release date set for autumn 2002. Nicole had enjoyed working with Hare on *The Blue Room* and had brought him a film project about artist Lee Miller. She was delighted that he was writing the script and that she was working with the director of *Billy Elliot*.

David wrote the most beautiful character for me. Judi Dench and I were talking the other day about how he's very difficult to learn because his sentence structure is unusual and you have to learn it word for word. You want to learn it properly. You really want to do it justice.

The film also starred Meryl Streep and Julianne Moore, and Daldry later commented that people didn't believe Nicole was in it because she was so heavily made-up and gave such a strong performance. Nicole was delighted at the opportunity to play Virginia Woolf: she did her customary intense research, Woolf's insights into human nature proving particularly appropriate for Nicole as she suffered through 2001.

This was a woman who grappled with death and madness and love, the big issues, and I'm very nervous to play her, but I also feel right now is such a wonderful time for me to play her because my emotions are so on the surface. Discovering her in

my 30s was when I needed to discover Virginia Woolf. Because I think you need to have some experiences in life, you need to have an intellectual capacity to handle Virginia, which you don't necessarily have – well, I didn't have – as a teenager. I was pretty nihilistic in terms of my view of what it was all about, where we were going. Why I was existing in the world, really. Why, was the big question. So it was sort of the perfect time to encounter Mrs Woolf. Because you're raw, emotionally raw. Your ability to understand with compassion somebody else's struggle is just there. ... It's cathartic, because it means you're not alone.

It wasn't an easy shoot physically for Nicole, although she was happy to undergo the make up sessions required for the role, even if her children started referring to her as "the Woolf woman" when they saw her wearing it. She refused to let a double do any takes in a cold, rushing river where the crew re-enacted Woolf's suicide. After shooting was completed, rather than let a double do last-minute close-ups of Woolf's hand as she wrote, she insisted on returning to London from the United States to shoot the scenes, learning to write right-handed.

But that's always been important to Nicole.

If you take on a role, you take it on. You don't have somebody else step in and do the hard bits.

TOP OF THE CHARTS

ABOVE: Problems? What problems? Nicole faces the press at the Cannes Film Festival in May 2001.

IT was probably the last thing Nicole needed. Amidst all the discussions with Cruise's lawyers over the divorce, and the continuing press interest in her future, she was also being stalked.

Just before she headed to Cannes in May, she filed for a temporary restraining order against Matthew E Hooker. Nicole claimed that the 40-year-old self-described screenwriter and poet "has come to my home on numerous occasions" and "threatened to commit acts of violence." Hooker allegedly believed he would make an ideal husband for Nicole and a good father to Isabella and Connor.

After attempting to contact Nicole with a hand-written note to her management company, he posted an "urgent and important message for Nicole" on his website in March stating that whoever it was who was sabotaging "any chance we have of being close" was providing her with advice that was "a horrible and illegal violation" of his rights. "You won't find a more wonderful man, a better soulmate, or a better husband. The fact that you have two lovely children doesn't bother me at all ... I'm ready to be a father to them." He said he would keep his message private for 48 hours if "you and Tom would be honest" and explain "confidentially, in private" why he was being rejected. The letter then signed off with "(Hopefully) yours, Nicole... Matt," and added: "Any future we might have together is at stake."

A week later, Hooker wrote offering to "tutor" the children, "to give us the chance to get to know each other." Then on 22 March, Nicole said, Hooker rang the call button at the gate of her Los Angeles home "at least eight times" and told her that he wanted to take her and the kids out for ice cream. Six days later, he came back "with a bouquet of flowers behind his back" and, over the intercom, allegedly told one of

Nicole's staff that he wanted to take Nicole to the ballet and that "she's playing hard to get." He then became aggressive when told to leave by security guards, saying, "This is between me and Nicole."

Hooker was eventually ordered to stay away from Nicole for three years, but in a bizarre postscript to the story, he filed a suit himself against Nicole in May 2002. Hooker demanded $15m because Nicole had been harassing him "for the express purpose of providing publicity" for herself, *Moulin Rouge!* and *The Others*. To add insult to injury, Hooker also demanded all the gross receipts from the two films!

The divorce process was also getting messy. Cruise's lawyer said that Nicole "has always known exactly why the parties are divorcing," despite her protestations that she didn't. Accusations and counter-accusations were flying around, while both parties maintained that their primary consideration was their children.

However, where work was concerned, they remained professional. Cruise produced *The Others*, Nicole starred in it – so there was no question of either of them missing the American premiere, even if it was on the day before their separation was formalised. Nicole carried out her commitments promoting the film, causing a commotion at the Venice Film Festival when the boat carrying her along the canals had to break the speed limit to get away from the pursuing paparazzi.

The tragedy at the World Trade Center on 11 September 2001 had a profound effect on both Cruise and Nicole. As high-profile Hollywood stars, they were honoured to form part of the major show put together in support of the disaster fund, *America: A Tribute to Heroes*. As human beings, it made them realise that they needed to get on with their lives.

When the attorneys met on 12 November, no one expected that there would be a speedy resolution. But there was. After just three hours, the papers were signed and, according to *People* magazine, "When it was done, Tom and Nicole actually hugged each other." Although Cruise won custody of their $28m Gulfstream jet, he agreed that Nicole could use it when she wanted to visit the children, or take them down to Australia. She won their $34m family home in Pacific Palisades and their home in Sydney. They shared custody of the children – Cruise would have them for Thanksgiving while Nicole spent Christmas with her children in Australia.

Nicole was already getting on with her life. *Moulin Rouge!* had opened up the possibility of a singing career for her and, in late August 2001, she got together with pop star Robbie Williams to collaborate on *Somethin' Stupid*, a track for his Rat Pack tribute album, *Swing When You're Winning*. Williams admitted that he was nervous.

When I was told I had a meeting with Nicole Kidman the arse fell out of my world. I was like, how am I going to get through this and not look like an idiot or try to lick her face?

Williams was surprised and pleased to discover that Nicole was just as nervous as he was when they got together at Capitol Studios to lay down the tracks. It was the start of a friendship that consolidated a new tabloid guessing game – who was Nicole Kidman's latest lover? Names such as Russell Crowe had been bandied around, although the press conveniently forgot that Crowe and Nicole had been friends for many years, spending many New Year's Eves together.

When Nicole ended up innocently spending the night in Robbie Williams' London hotel suite a few weeks later, during filming of the video to accompany the single, she felt obliged to comment:

Robbie and I have become good friends – that's all ... It's not what people might think, but Robbie is irresistible because he is so much fun to be around. He's a very funny man.

Somethin' Stupid was the icing on the cake for the most unusual year of Nicole Kidman's life. Who would have thought that she would end up as Number One in the UK charts?

As 2001 came to a close, *In The Cut* went through further changes. Although reports that Nicole wouldn't star in as well as produce the movie had been denied during the summer, at the start of 2002 they were confirmed. Filming began in July 2002.

While that was being sorted out, Nicole achieved another of her aims: working with experimental director Lars von Trier on the movie *Dogville*. Although it had seemed that negotiations had broken down between Nicole and von Trier's production company, the director was delighted to announce in July 2001 that Nicole would be part of the company for the film. *Dogville* was shot over a period of six weeks and Nicole found that once again she was working with a director who valued her input.

Dogville was set in a mountain village in America, although it was shot in the Swedish village of Trollhattan. The film's style was very unusual – there were no props, and the town was indicated by chalk marks on the floor of the sound stage.

We wanted to make a film where you take the walls away in society and how you can actually see everybody doing their business as if they were in town. So all the actors had to be there all the time. The dog in the film is actually the chalk mark, and we all sort of go and pat the dog – but the dog is just a chalk mark. It's either going to work or it's going to be a disaster.

Even after completing the movie, Nicole was nervous about the outcome. She wasn't certain that she had been in the right frame of mind for filming the pretty harrowing script, but she had confidence in von Trier. Director and star would go for long walks in the snowy forests around the studio, and Nicole found that these helped her inestimably. Even if she was depressed by what was going on in the rest of her life, Nicole kept everyone happy during the shooting of *Dogville*. Her co-star Paul Bettany said that although Trolhattan was the dullest place on Earth, Nicole managed to "make it a ball". She arranged for oysters and Cristal champagne to be delivered to the set, and even managed to persuade Bettany to accompany her on hikes around the mountains, scaring him with campfire stories until they both had to run miles to get back to their car because they had scared themselves so much.

Working on such a small project kept Nicole's feet on the ground at a time when everyone else was praising her to the skies. Although she had made a brief cameo appearance as an Academy Award presenter as a favour for her old friend John Duigan in his 1996 film *The Leading Man*, Nicole had never been honoured by the prestigious Academy herself. Although an Oscar itself was still to elude her, *Moulin Rouge!* and *The Others* were nominated for many awards and prizes, including Nicole's first Academy Award nomination for *Moulin Rouge!*. She bagged a Golden Globe, a Golden Satellite, an Empire and two MTV awards, as well as the London Film Critics' accolade as Actress of the Year for *Moulin Rouge!*, and a Saturn Award for *The Others*. It seemed as if the effects of 2001 would resonate with Nicole for many years to come.

INTO THE FUTURE

AFTER completing work on *Dogville*, Nicole joined Ed Harris and *Billy Bathgate* director Robert Benton on *The Human Stain*, playing Anthony Hopkins' troubled young mistress, Faunia. Once again, Nicole threw herself into the research for the character, a cleaning lady with an abusive past. She met with Philip Roth, the author of the book on which the film was based, who filled in the background of the woman, and directed her towards various women's shelters. Nicole was affected by the experience, and promised the women that above all else, she would give Faunia dignity. She was really touched when the abused women asked her also to show that they had not brought the abuse upon themselves.

Once *The Human Stain* had wrapped, Nicole travelled to Romania to shoot the romantic drama *Cold Mountain*, alongside Jude Law, Renée Zellwegger and Natalie Portman, directed by *The Talented Mr Ripley*'s Anthony Minghella from a novel by Charles Frazier. The film is set during the American Civil War, and Nicole's preparation included finding out about the way of life during that period, and learning to play Chopin on the piano. She was looking forward to playing the role of Ada after the tragic characters of Woolf and Faunia.

To play Ada at the end of all this is so lovely, because it's about hope, it's about belief, it's about people coming out for each other in a time of crisis. There is cruelty in human nature, but I've seen the evidence of great kindness as well.

As the year drew to a close, Nicole gave various interviews to promote the release of *The Hours* before taking a prolonged family holiday. In February 2003, she is set to reunite with Lauren Bacall on the dramatic mystery *Birth*, directed by Jonathan Glazer. *Birth* follows the story of a 10-year-old boy who falls in love with an older woman, played by Nicole. He then becomes convinced that he is the reincarnation of the woman's late husband, causing her to question her past. Bacall will play Nicole's mother

Once that's completed, Nicole plans to have "some fun" in the remake of the Seventies science fiction movie *The Stepford Wives* from director Frank Oz. Her name has also been linked to a big screen remake of the classic sixties TV series, *Bewitched*, with Nicole taking the role of witch Samantha Stephens made famous by Elizabeth Montgomery.

Nicole has said that she wants to work with directors like Martin Scorsese, Steven Spielberg and the Serbian filmmaker Emir Kusturica. Big-budget films don't usually interest her, unless they offer something that she wouldn't get elsewhere.

I get to reach out to a whole lot of people with ideas, sometimes profound ideas, and sometimes they work and sometimes they don't. But you still get to work with some of the most brilliant people in the world, and you help to facilitate extraordinary ideas. So I consider myself incredibly fortunate to be working with these people.

She's been linked romantically with a number of Hollywood names – from *Spider-Man*'s Tobey Maguire to Russell Crowe. She deflects the questions with practised ease. Only Nicole really knows who her affections are devoted to outside of her immediate family. It wasn't until the autumn of 2002 that she started to think of herself as divorced, because she saw the breakdown of her marriage as a failure on her part.

BELOW:
Nicole at the Critics Choice Awards in Los Angeles, January 2003

If you ask what I would have loved for my life, it's not this. I would have loved to emulate my parents, for my marriage to have been successful, to have raised my children within that cocoon. But now I'm a divorced woman, along with millions of other divorced women. Grappling with all that that entails.

Her priority remains her children. She's determined that she will not become a victim as a result of what's happened to her, and that her children will grow up to be the best people they can be. She knows she has the love of her family and friends, without which she couldn't have coped. But whatever comes Nicole Kidman's way, she will face it, accept it – and make it the best it can be.

My present situation is strange and bizarre and all of those things, but it is what it is. It's not what it should have been, not what it could have been. It is what it is. I'm not sure what the future holds but I do know that I'm going to be positive and not wake up feeling desperate.

One of the things I've had to grapple with is just who am I, where do I fit in now in the world if I'm not with my partner anymore. That's where you sort of try and put your two feet on the ground and go, 'OK, I'm going to take my steps forward – alone.'"

I think with the divorce, I really grew up. Prior to that, I was walking around with rose-coloured glasses. I always knew in the back of my head that everybody has to deal with something bad in this life. To deal with it all in the space of a couple of months though was like, 'Ugh, this is too much, how am I ever, ever, ever going to live through this?' But then I did, and that's when I went, 'I think I've grown up now.'

For Nicole Kidman, the sky now really is the limit.

FILMOGRAPHY

1983

CHASE THROUGH THE NIGHT

ABC/Independent Productions

114 mins

Producer: Brendon Lunney; Director: Howard Rubie; Writer: Rob George (based on a book by Max Fatchen); Cinematography: Ernest Clark

Cast: Brett Climo (Ray), Alan Dargin (Bindaree), Nicole Kidman (Petra), John Jarratt (Clurry), Scott McGregor (Yorkie), Paul Sonkkila (Darby), Lyn Collingwood (Mrs Y), Steve Dodd (Narli), Justine Saunders (Mary), Ron Blanchard (Mert), Roger Cox (Bill Ky), Jeff Truman (Eric), Stu Cochrane (Jack), Brian Hinzlewood (Max), Pam Western (Mavis)

BUSH CHRISTMAS

aka *Prince and the Great Race*

Australian Film Commission, Barron Entertainment Ltd., Bush Christmas Productions Pty. Ltd., Film and Television Institute, W.A., Queensland Film Corporation

91 mins

Producers: Gilda Baracchi, Paul D Barron; Director: Henri Safran; Writer: Ted Roberts; Cinematography: Ross Berryman and Malcolm Richards

Cast: John Ewart (Bill), John Howard (Sly), Mark Spain (John Thompson), James Wingrove (Michael), Peter Summer (Ben Thompson), Nicole Kidman (Helen), Manalpuy (Manalpuy), Vineta O'Malley (Kate Thompson), Maurice Hughes (Carrol), Bob Hunt (Jack), Brian Thompson (Bookmaker), Liam Maloney (Derby Mulcahy)

BMX BANDITS

aka *Shortwave*

Nilsen Premiere/MNTEX Entertainment

88 mins

Producers: Tom Broadbridge, Brian Burgess, Paul F Davies; Director: Brian Trenchard - Smith; Writers: Patrick Edgeworth, Russell Hagg; Cinematography: John Seale

Cast: David Argue (Whitey), John Ley (Moustache), Nicole Kidman (Judy), Angelo D'Angelo (PJ), James Lugton (Goose), Bryan Marshall (The Boss), Brian Sloman (The Creep), Peter Browne (Police constable), Bill Brady (Police sergeant), Linda Newton (Policewoman)

1984

MATTHEW AND SON

Ten Network

75 mins

Producer: Damien Parer; Director: Gary Conway; Writers: Marcus Cole, Bert Deling; Cinematography: Ellery Ryan

Cast: Douglas Bennett (Mr. Hutchins), Paul Cronin (Matthew Caine), Paula Duncan (Barbara Dean), Greg Fleet (Jim Finn), Regina Gaigalas (Kate Trehearn), Caroline Gillmer (Gloria Doran), Mark Hennessy (Drug Addict), Edward Hepple (Bert Macrostie), Telford Jackson (Magistrate), Effie James (Mrs. Brindley), Victor Kazan (Neville Jackson), Nicole Kidman (Bridget Elliot), Peter Kowitz (Jerry Ashton), Jay Mannering (Max), Alethea McGrath (Minnie Timmins), Alex Menglet (Gebhard), John Murphy (Mr Brindley), Darius Perkins (Stephen Caine), Ron Pinnell (Caretaker), Marie Redshaw (Gloria Doran), Andrew Thompson (Kev), Peter West (Stan)

FIVE MILE CREEK
Disney / Channel 7 Network
24 x 46 mins episodes

Producer: Henry Crawford; Directors: Frank
Arnold, Gary Conway, Kevin James Dobson,
Michael Jenkins, Brendan Maher, George
Miller, Rob Stewart, Brian Trenchard-Smith;
Writers: David Boutland, Tom Hegarty, Peter
A Kinloch, Gwenda Marsh, Greg Millin,
Denise Morgan, Keith Thompson;
Cinematography: Kevan Lind

Cast: Louise Caire Clark (Maggie Scott),
Rod Mullinar (Jack Taylor), Liz Burch
(Kate Wallace), Michael Caton (Paddy
Malone), Priscilla Weems (Hannah Scott),
Martin Lewis (Sam), Gus Mercurio (Ben
Jones), Jay Kerr (Con Madigan), Peter Carroll
(Charles Withers), Nicole Kidman (Annie),
Shannon Presby (Matt)

1985
WINNERS
aka *Room to Move* [syndication title]
Australian Children's Television
Foundation / ITC
8 x 30 minute episodes plus
TV Movie compilation

Executive Producer: Patricia Edgar;
Producers: Richard Mason, Julia Overton;
Director: John Duigan: Writer: John Duigan;
Cinematography: Michael Edols

Cast: Nicole Kidman (Carol Trig), Alyssa-
Jane Cook (Angie Spry), Terence Donovan
(Peter Trig), Veronica Lang (Alison Trig),
Martin Harris (Bruce Spry), Emma Lyle
(Andrea Trig), Helen Pankhurst (Jenny
Forenko), Mary Sinclair (Mrs Gravy), Kate
Ferguson (Sandar Wilcox), Celia De Burgh
(Lucy Graham), Carla Hoogeveen (Mrs
MacCreedy), Mitsuko Generoso (Dance
Teacher), Mercia Deane-Johns (Janet), Shirley
Cameron (Michelle Guest), Elizabeth Mavric

(Stephany), Angela Gauci (Tracey), Connor
Fitzpatrick (Andrew), Matthew Parr
(Gilmore), John Pallone (Tony), Adrian
Thompson (Ollie), Vic Andrews (Mario),
Gary Dale (1st Policeman), Ian Gilmour
(2nd Policeman), Esben Storm (Tom),
Robert Underhill (Ian), Robbie Campbell
(Ross), Chris Dibb (Businessman)

WILLS & BURKE
aka *The Wacky World of Wills & Burke*
McDonald / Weis
100 mins

Producers: Margot McDonald,
Bob Weis; Director: Bob Weis;
Writer: Philip Dalkin; Cinematography:
Nino Gaetano Martinetti

Cast: Garry McDonald (Robert O'Hara
Burke), Kym Gyngell (William John Wills),
Peter Collingwood (Sir William Stawell),
Jonathan Hardy (John Macadam), Roderick
Williams (George Landells), Mark Little
(John King), Roy Baldwin (Charley Gray),
Alex Menglet (William Brahe), Tony Rickards
(Patton), Simon Thorpe (McDonough),
Wyn Roberts (William Wright), Dalibor
Satalic (Beckler), Nicole Kidman (Julia
Matthews), Henry Maas (Charles), Chris
Haywood (Constable), Kirk Alexander Mr
Lewis), Stephen Kearney (Ambrose), Neill
Gladwin (Godfrey), Colin Hay (Publican),
Mark Mitchell (Carpenter), Jay Mannering
(Menindee local), Andrew Martin (Welch),
Paul Kuek (Father)

ARCHER'S ADVENTURE
aka *Archer*
Ten Network / Roadshow
95 mins

Producer: Moya Iceton; Director: Denny
Lawrence; Writer: Anne Brooksbank;
Cinematography: Frank Hammond

Cast: Brett Climo (Dave Power), Ernie Gray (Matthew Swift), John Flaus (Egan), Ned Lander (Jack Cutts), Tony Barry (Squatter), Paul Bertram (Lord Alfred), Robert Coleby (Etienne de Mestre), Nicole Kidman (Catherine), Anna Maria Monticelli (Anna Swift)

1986
WINDRIDER
Bush Christmas Productions
92 mins

Producer: Paul D Barron; Director: Vincent Monton; Writers: Everett De Roche, Bonnie Harris; Cinematography: Joseph Pickering.

Cast: Tom Burlinson (P C Simpson), Nicole Kidman (Jade), Jill Perryman (Miss Dodge), Charles 'Bud' Tingwell (Stewart Simpson Sr), Simon Chilvers (Howard), Kim Bullad (Coyote), Stig Wemyss (Ratso), Mark Williams (Mangles), Alastair Cummings (Rabbit), Robin Miller (Wally), Matt Parkinson (Lurch), Lorraine Webster (Mud), John Ryan (McBride), Lance Karapetcoff (King), Ric Whittle (Ross), Andy Copeman (Hayes), Trevor Spencer (Engineer), Alistair Browning (Cram), Penny Brown (Kate)

WATCH THE SHADOWS DANCE
aka *Nightmaster*
Somerset Films
91 mins

Producers: Jan Tyrrell, James Michael Vernon; Director: Mark Joffe; Writer: Michael McGennan; Cinematography: Martin McGrath

Cast: Tom Jennings (Robby Mason), Nicole Kidman (Amy Gabriel), Joanne Samuel (Sonia Spane), Vince Martin (Steve Beck), Craig Pearce (Guy Duncan), Doug Parkinson (Pete 'Pearly' Gates), Jeremy

Shadlow (Simon), Alexander Broun (Henry), Laurence Clifford (Brian Simmons), Paul Gleeson (Peter Hastings), Mark Hennessy (Aloysius Askew), James Lugton (Tote 'Ali' Bent), Chris Truswell ('Fingers' Hough), Terry Brady (Lieutenant Trout), Richard Jones (Gary Garter), Linda Megier (Kelly), Allen Leong (Luis), Sean Garlick (Stave Opponent), Brett A'Hearn (Karate Contestant), Nicholas Jeanes (Well-dressed Man), Teresa Jennings (Mrs Mason)

VIETNAM
Kennedy Miller Productions
10 x 50 min episodes

Producers: Terry Hayes, George Miller, Doug Mitchell; Directors: John Duigan, Chris Noonan; Writers: John Duigan, Terry Hayes, Chris Noonan; Cinematography: Geoff Burton.

Cast: Alan Cassell, Pauline Chan (Lien), Brett Climo (Ritchie), Mick Conway (Knifethrower), Alyssa-Jane Cook (Deb), Celia De Burgh (Monica Montgomery), Nicholas Eadie (Phil Goddard), Noel Ferrier (Sir Robert Menzies), Lucky Grills (Sen. Shane Paltridge), Jim Holt (Lt Smart), Nicole Kidman (Megan Goddard), Veronica Lang (Evelyn Goddard), Mark Lee (Laurie Fellows), Barry Otto (Douglas Goddard), Grace Parr (Le), Jay Patterson (Marty), John Polson (Serge), Don Reid (Paul Hasluck), Daniel Rigney (Soldier (uncredited)), Tim Robertson (Pascoe), Henri Szeps (Harold Holt)

1987
THE BIT PART
Comedia Ltd.
87 mins

Executive Producer: Steve Vizard; Producers: John Gauci, Peter Herbert; Director: Brendan

Maher; Writers: Peter Herbert, Ian McFaden, Steve Vizard; Cinematography: Ellery Ryan. Cast: Chris Haywood (Michael Thornton), Katrina Foster (Helen Thornton), Nicole Kidman (Mary McAllister), John Wood (John Bainbridge), Maurie Fields (Peter), Brian Mannix (Barry), Deborra-Lee Furness (Acting Teacher), Ian McFadyen (Commercial Director), Maggie Millar (Molly), Maureen Edwards (Bev Howard), Wilbur Wilde (Bikie), Red Symons (Bikie), Des McKenna (Bikie), Kirk Alexander (Andy), John Allan (Steve), Reg Gorman (Scott), Lou Carr (Bernie), Maud Clark (Felicity), Christopher Mayer (David), Kate Jason (Sara), Peter Felmingham (Paul), Isabell Ryan (Dance Teacher), Earl Francis (Arthur), Luciano Catenacci (Mario)

UN' AUSTRALIANA A ROMA

Australian Broadasting Company
Producer: Luciano Martino; Director: Sergio Martino; Screenplay: Luciano Martino

Cast: Nicole Kidman (Jill)
with Massimo Ciavarro

1988

EMERALD CITY

Limelight Productions / New South Wales Film Corp
92 mins

Producer: Joan Long; Director: Michael Jenkins; Writer: David Williamson (based on his play); Cinematography: Paul Murphy

Cast: John Hargreaves (Colin Rogers), Robyn Nevin (Kate Rogers), Chris Haywood (Mike McCord), Nicole Kidman (Helen), Ruth Cracknell (Elaine Ross), Dennis Miller (Malcolm Bennett), Nicholas Hammond (Ian Wall), Ella Scott (Penny Rogers), Haydon Samuels (Sam Rogers), Michelle Torres (Kath McCall)

1989

DEAD CALM

Warner Bros
95 mins

Producers: Terry Hayes, George Miller, Doug Mitchell; Director: Phillip Noyce; Writer: Terry Hayes (from the original novel by Charles Williams); Cinematography: Dean Semler with Ross Berryman and Geoff Burton

Cast: Nicole Kidman (Rae Ingram), Sam Neill (John Ingram), Billy Zane (Hughie Warriner), Rod Mullinar (Russell Bellows), Joshua Tilden (Danny), George Shevtsov (Doctor), Michael Long (Specialist Doctor), Lisa Collins ('Orpheus' Cruise Girl), Paula Hudson-Brinkley ('Orpheus' Cruise Girl), Sharon Cook ('Orpheus' Cruise Girl), Malinda Rutter ('Orpheus' Cruise Girl)

BANGKOK HILTON

Kennedy Miller Productions
240 mins [2 x 120 minutes]

Producer: Terry Hayes, George Miller, Doug Mitchell; Director: Ken Cameron; Writer: Terry Hayes (from a story by Ken Cameron and Tony Morphett); Cinematography: Geoff Burton

Cast: Nicole Kidman (Katrina Stanton), Denholm Elliott (Hal Stanton), Hugo Weaving (Richard Carlisle), Joy Smithers (Mandy Engels), Norman Kaye (George McNair), Jerome Ehlers (Arkie Ragan), Pauline Chan (Pretty Warder), Noah Taylor (Billy Engels), Richard Carter (Detective King), Gerda Nicolson (Lady Faulkner), Judy Morris (Catherine Faulkner)

FLIRTING
Kennedy Miller Productions
99 mins

Producers: Terry Hayes, George Miller, Doug
Mitchell; Director: John Duigan; Writer: John
Duigan; Cinematography: Geoff Burton.

Cast: Noah Taylor (Danny Embling),
Thandie Newton (Thandiwe Adjewa),
Nicole Kidman (Nicola Radcliffe),
Bartholomew Rose ('Gilby' Fryer), Felix
Nobis (Jock Blair), Josh Picker ('Backa'
Bourke), Kiri Paramore ('Slag' Green),
Marc Gray (Christopher Laidlaw), Gregg
Palmer (Colin Proudfoot), Joshua Marshall
('Cheddar' Fedderson), David Wieland
('Possum' Piper), Craig Black ('Pup'
Pierdon), Les Hill (Greg Gilmore), Jeff
Truman (Mr Morris Cutts), Marshall Napier
(Mr Rupert Elliott), John Dicks (Rev Consti
Nicholson), Kym Wilson (Melissa Miles),
Naomi Watts (Janet Odgers), Lisa Spinadel
(Barbara Howe), Francesca Raft (Fiona Spry),
Louise Hannan (Theresa Bradley), Danielle
Lyttleton (Jean Thomas), Jacqui Fifer (Stacey
Burt), Fiona Press (Mrs Archer), Maggie
Blinco (Miss Guinevere MacReady), Jane
Harders (Miss Sylvia Anderson), Malcolm
Robertson (Bruce Embling), Judi Farr (Shella
Embling), Freddie Paris (Solomon Adjewa),
Femi Taylor (Letitia Adjewa), Gillian Hyde
(Dr. Alison Pierce), Harry Lawrence (Motel
Manager), Michael Williams (Sonny Liston),
Kurt Frey (Jean-Paul Sartre)

1990

DAYS OF THUNDER
Paramount Pictures
107 mins

Executive Producer: Gerald R Molen;
Producers: Jerry Bruckheimer, Don Simpson;
Director: Tony Scott; Writer: Robert Towne
(from a story by Robert Towne and Tom
Cruise); Cinematography: Ward Russell

Cast: Tom Cruise (Cole Trickle), Robert
Duvall (Harry Hogge), Nicole Kidman (Dr
Claire Lewicki), Randy Quaid (Tim Daland),
Cary Elwes (Russ Wheeler), Michael Rooker
(Rowdy Burns), Fred Dalton Thompson (Big
John), John C Reilly (Buck Bretherton), J C
Quinn (Waddell), Don Simpson (Aldo
Bennedetti), Caroline Williams (Jennie
Burns), Donna Wilson (Darlene), Chris Ellis
(Harlem Hoogerhyde), John Griesemer (Len
Dortort), Barbara Garrick (Lauren Daland),
Gerald R Molen (Dr. Wilhaire) [as Jerry
Molen], Margo Martindale (Donna), Jim
Crowther (Dr Crowther), James D Henson
(Doctor) [as James D Henson MD], Jerry
Punch (himself) [as Dr Jerry Punch], Neil
Bonnett (himself), Harry P Gant (himself),
Rusty Wallace (himself), Richard Petty
(himself) [uncredited]

1991

BILLY BATHGATE
Touchstone / Buena Vista
106 mins

Producers: Robert F Colesberry,
Arlene Donovan; Director: Robert Benton;
Writer: Tom Stoppard (from the book by
E L Doctorow); Cinematography:
Néstor Almendros

Cast: Dustin Hoffman (Dutch Schultz),
Nicole Kidman (Drew Preston), Loren Dean
(Billy Bathgate), Bruce Willis (Bo Weinberg),
Steven Hill (Otto Berman), Steve Buscemi
(Irving), Billy Jaye (Mickey), John Costelloe
(Lulu), Timothy Jerome (Dixie Davis),
Stanley Tucci (Lucky Luciano), Mike Starr
(Julie Martin), Robert F Colesberry (Jack
Kelly), Stephen Joyce (Mr Hines), Frances
Conroy (Mary Behan), Moira Kelly (Becky),
Kevin Corrigan (Arnold), Xander Berkeley
(Harvey Preston), Barry McGovern (Father
McInemy), Richard Bekins (Carter),
Katharine Houghton (Charlotte), Robert D
Raiford (Judge), Terry Loughlin (Mr Chambers)

1992

FAR AND AWAY
Universal Pictures
140 mins

Executive Producer: Todd Hallowell;
Producers: Brian Grazer and Ron Howard;
Director: Ron Howard; Writer: Bob Dolman
(from a story by Bob Dolman and Ron
Howard); Cinematography: Mikael Salomon

Cast: Tom Cruise (Joseph Donnelly),
Nicole Kidman (Shannon Christie),
Thomas Gibson (Steven), Robert Prosky
(Daniel Christie), Barbara Babcock (Nora
Christie), Cyril Cusack (Danty Duff), Eileen
Pollock (Molly Kay), Colm Meaney (Kelly),
Douglas Gillison (Dermody), Michelle
Johnson (Grace), Wayne Grace (Bourke),
Niall Toibin (Joe), Barry McGovern
(McGuire), Gary Lee Davis (Gordon), Jared
Harris (Paddy), Steve O'Donnell (Colm),
Peadar Lamb (Farmer), Wesley Murphy
(Landlord), Jimmy Keogh (Priest), Derry
Power (Peter), Noel O'Donovan (Matthew),
Macdara O'Fatharta (John), Clint Howard
(Flynn), Jeffrey Andrews (Coniff), Judith
McIntyre (Glenna), Rynagh O'Grady (Olive)

1993

MALICE
Columbia Pictures
107 mins

Executive Producers: Michael Hirsh, Patrick
Loubert; Producers: Harold Becker, Charles
Mulvehill, Rachel Pfeffer; Director: Harold
Becker; Writers: Aaron Sorkin and Scott
Frank (from a story by Aaron Sorkin and
Jonas McCord); Cinematography: Gordon Willis

Cast: Alec Baldwin (Dr Jed Hill), Nicole
Kidman (Tracy Kennsinger), Bill Pullman
(Andy Safian), Bebe Neuwirth (Dana),
George C Scott (Dr Kessler), Anne Bancroft
(Mrs Kennsinger), Peter Gallagher (Dennis
Riley), Josef Sommer (Lester Adams), Tobin
Bell (Earl Leemus), William Duff-Griffin
(Dr George Sullivan), Debrah Farentino
(Tanya), Gwyneth Paltrow (Paula Bell),
David Bowe (Dr Matthew Robertson),
Diana Bellamy (Ms Worthington)

MY LIFE
Columbia Pictures
117 mins

Executive Producer: Gil Netter; Producers:
Bruce Joel Rubin, Hunt Lowry, Jerry Zucker;
Director: Bruce Joel Rubin; Writer: Bruce Joel
Rubin; Cinematography: Peter James

Cast: Michael Keaton (Bob Jones), Nicole Kidman
(Gail Jones), Bradley Whitford (Paul Ivanovich),
Queen Latifah (Theresa), Michael Constantine
(Bill), Rebecca Schull (Rose), Mark Lowenthal
(Dr Hills), Lee Garlington (Carol Sandman),
Toni Sawyer (Doris), Haing S Ngor (Mr Ho), Romy
Rosemont (Anya Stasiuk), Danny Rimmer (Young
Bobbie), Ruth de Sosa (Young Rose), Richard Schiff
(Young Bill), Stephen Taylor Knot (Young Paul),
Andrew Camuccio (Baby Brian), Brian Camuccio
(Baby Brian), Colby Sawyer Garabedian (Little Boy
Brian), Mary Ann Thebus (Miss Morgenstern),
Brenda Strong (Laura), Rudi Davis (George), Mark
Holton (Sam), Lissa Walters (Deborah), Bruce
Jarchow (Walter), Jane Morris (Dorothy), Kenneth
Tigar (Dr Califano), Ray Reinhardt (Dr Altman),
Frank DiElsi (Arnold Sherman), Billy L Sullivan
(Rollercoaster Boy), Michael Gallagher
(Rollercoaster Friend), Christopher Miranda
(Rollercoaster Friend), Nora Taylor (Little
Girl), Dianne B Shaw (Detroit Mother),
Sondra Rubin (Aunt Sophia), Sylvia Kauders
(Aunt Tekla), Sharon Conley (Lida Stasiuk),
James R Sweeney (Nestor Stasiuk), Vasek
Simek (Uncle Henry), Magda Harout
(Aunt Sonia), Mark Zingale (Delivery Man),
Jonathan Fish (Delivery Man), James Rubin
(Uncle Jimmy), Jennifer Flackett
(Childbirth Teacher)

1995

BATMAN FOREVER
Warner Bros
122 mins

Executive Producers: Michael E Uslan, Benjamin Melniker; Producers: Tim Burton, Peter MacGregor-Scott; Director: Joel Schumacher; Writers: Lee Batchler, Janet Scott Batchler and Akiva Goldsman (from a story by Lee Batchler and Janet Scott Batchler; characters created by Bob Kane); Cinematography: Stephen Goldblatt

Cast: Val Kilmer (Batman/Bruce Wayne), Tommy Lee Jones (Harvey Two-Face/Harvey Dent), Jim Carrey (The Riddler/Edward Nygma), Nicole Kidman (Dr Chase Meridien), Chris O'Donnell (Robin/Dick Grayson), Michael Gough (Alfred Pennyworth), Pat Hingle (Commissioner Gordon), Drew Barrymore (Sugar), Debi Mazar (Spice), Elizabeth Sanders (Gossip Gerty), Rene Auberjonois (Dr Burton, at Arkham Asylum), Joe Grifasi (Bank Guard), Philip Moon (Newscaster), Jessica Tuck (Female Newscaster), Dennis Paladino (Crime Boss Moroni), Kimberly Scott (Margaret, Wayne's assistant), Michael Paul Chan (Executive), Jon Favreau (Assistant), Greg Lauren (Aide), Ramsey Ellis (Young Bruce Wayne), Michael Scranton (Thomas Wayne), Eileen Seeley (Martha Wayne), David U Hodges (Shooter), Jack Betts (Fisherman), Tim Jackson (Municipal Police Guard), Daniel Reichert (Ringmaster), Glory Fioramonti (Mom Grayson), Larry A Lee (Dad Grayson), Bruce Roberts (Handsome Reporter), George Wallace (Mayor), Bob Zmuda (Electronic Store Owner)

TO DIE FOR
Columbia/Sony Pictures
106 mins

Executive Producer: Joseph M Caracciolo, Jonathan T Taplin; Producer: Laura Ziskin; Director: Gus Van Sant; Writer: Buck Henry (based on the book by Joyce Maynard); Cinematography: Eric Alan Edwards

Cast: Nicole Kidman (Suzanne Stone Maretto), Matt Dillon (Larry Maretto), Joaquin Phoenix (Jimmy Emmett), Casey Affleck (Russel Hines), Illeana Douglas (Janice Maretto), Alison Folland (Lydia Mertz), Dan Hedaya (Joe Maretto), Wayne Knight (Ed Grant), Kurtwood Smith (Earl Stone), Holland Taylor (Carol Stone), Susan Traylor (Faye Stone), Maria Tucci (Angela Maretto), Tim Hopper (Mike Warden), Michael Rispoli (Ben DeLuca), Buck Henry (Mr H Finlaysson), Gerry Quigley (George), Tom Forrester (Fisherman), Alan Edward Lewis (Fisherman), Nadine MacKinnon (Sexy Woman), Conrad Coates (Weaselly Guy), Ron Gabriel (Sal), Ian Heath (Student), Graeme Millington (Student), Sean Ryan (Student), Nicholas Pasco (Detective), Joyce Maynard (Lawyer), David Collins (Reporter), Eve Crawford (Reporter), Janet Lo (Reporter), David Cronenberg (Man at lake), Tom Quinn (Skating Promoter), Peter Glenn (Priest), Amber-Lee Campbell (Suzanne age 5), Colleen Williams (Valerie Mertz), Simon Richards (Chester), Philip Williams (Babe Hines), Susan Backs (June Hines), Kyra Harper (Mary Emmett), Adam Roth (Band Member), Andrew Scott (Band Member), Tamara Gorski (Chick #2 at Bar), Katie Griffin (Girl at Bar), Carla Renee (Girl at Bar)